He speaks to the horses.

Gee up, my boys! And on you go!
There's food ahead and fair stables,
315 for the monks are kind. Put the miles behind!

The creaking and rattling of the waggon, and the sound of hoofs, continue
for some time, during which no words are spoken. After a while lights glimmer
in the distance. Torhthelm speaks from the waggon, drowsily and half dreaming.

Tor. There are candles in the dark and cold voices.
I hear mass chanted for master's soul
in Ely isle. Thus ages pass,
and men after men. Mourning voices
320 of weeping women. So the world passes;
day follows day, and the dust gathers,
and his tomb crumbles, as time gnaws it,
and his kith and kindred out of ken dwindle.
So men flicker and in the mirk go out.
325 The world withers, and the wind rises;
the candles are quenched. Cold falls the night.

The lights disappear as he speaks. Torhthelm's voice becomes louder,
but is still the voice of one speaking in a dream.

It's dark! It's dark, and doom coming!
Is no light left us? A light kindle,
and fan the flame! Lo! fire awakens;   (fire now)
330 the hearth is burning, the house is lit, lighted,
and there men gather, out of the mists coming
through darkling doors whereat doom waiteth.
Hark! I hear them in the hall chanting:
stern words they sing with strong voices.

He chants: Let heart be prouder, harder be purpose,
335 more stern the will, as our strength weakens!
Mind shall not falter nor mood waver,
though doom shall come and dark conquer.

There is a great bump and jolt of the cart.

Hey! what a bump, Tída! My bones are shaken,
340 and my dream's shattered. It's dark and cold.

Tíd. Ay, a bump on the bone is bad for dreams,
and it's cold waking. But your words were queer,
Totta my lad, with your talk of wind,
and doom conquering and a dark ending.
345 It sounded fey and fell-hearted,
and heathenish, too : I don't hold with that.
It's night right enough ; but there's no firelight :
dark is over all, and dead is master.
When morning comes, it'll be much like others :
350 more labour and loss till the land's ruined ;
ever work and war till the world passes.

Torhthelm/

355 Heart shall be bolder, harder be purpose,
356 More proud our spirit as our power lessens   more strong the spirit as our strength lessens

THE BATTLE OF MALDON

Works by J.R.R. Tolkien

THE HOBBIT
LEAF BY NIGGLE
ON FAIRY-STORIES
FARMER GILES OF HAM
THE HOMECOMING OF BEORHTNOTH
THE LORD OF THE RINGS
THE ADVENTURES OF TOM BOMBADIL
THE ROAD GOES EVER ON (WITH DONALD SWANN)
SMITH OF WOOTTON MAJOR

Works published posthumously

SIR GAWAIN AND THE GREEN KNIGHT, PEARL AND SIR ORFEO*
THE FATHER CHRISTMAS LETTERS
THE SILMARILLION*
PICTURES BY J.R.R. TOLKIEN*
UNFINISHED TALES*
THE LETTERS OF J.R.R. TOLKIEN*
FINN AND HENGEST
MR BLISS
THE MONSTERS AND THE CRITICS & OTHER ESSAYS*
ROVERANDOM
THE CHILDREN OF HÚRIN*
THE LEGEND OF SIGURD AND GUDRÚN*
THE FALL OF ARTHUR*
BEOWULF: A TRANSLATION AND COMMENTARY*
THE STORY OF KULLERVO
THE LAY OF AOTROU AND ITROUN
BEREN AND LÚTHIEN*
THE FALL OF GONDOLIN*
THE NATURE OF MIDDLE-EARTH
THE FALL OF NÚMENOR

The History of Middle-earth – by Christopher Tolkien

I THE BOOK OF LOST TALES, PART ONE
II THE BOOK OF LOST TALES, PART TWO
III THE LAYS OF BELERIAND
IV THE SHAPING OF MIDDLE-EARTH
V THE LOST ROAD AND OTHER WRITINGS
VI THE RETURN OF THE SHADOW
VII THE TREASON OF ISENGARD
VIII THE WAR OF THE RING
IX SAURON DEFEATED
X MORGOTH'S RING
XI THE WAR OF THE JEWELS
XII THE PEOPLES OF MIDDLE-EARTH

* Edited by Christopher Tolkien

The Battle of Maldon

together with

The Homecoming of Beorhtnoth
Beorhthelm's Son

and

'The Tradition of Versification
in Old English'

Edited by Peter Grybauskas

HarperCollins*Publishers*

HarperCollins*Publishers* Ltd
1 London Bridge Street
London SE1 9GF

HarperCollins*Publishers*
Macken House, 39/40 Mayor Street Upper,
Dublin 1 D01 C9W8
Ireland

www.tolkien.co.uk
www.tolkienestate.com

First published by HarperCollins*Publishers* 2023

2

The facsimile manuscript page that appears as the frontispiece to this book
is reproduced courtesy of The Bodleian Library, University of Oxford, and is
selected from their holdings labelled MS Tolkien 5 folio 86r

A CIP catalogue record for this book is available from the British Library

ISBN 978–0–00–846582–7

Printed and bound in the UK using 100% renewable electricity at CPI Group (UK) Ltd

MIX
Paper | Supporting
responsible forestry
FSC
www.fsc.org FSC™ C007454

This book is produced from independently certified FSC™ paper
to ensure responsible forest management.

For more information visit: www.harpercollins.co.uk/green

CONTENTS

FOREWORD

'Coming home dead without a head (as Beorhtnoth did) is not very delightful'. So Tolkien quipped to his publishers Allen & Unwin in 1961, quite aptly capturing the gist of *The Homecoming of Beorhtnoth* (hereafter referred to as *The Homecoming*), while voicing his frustration about a glib description of the poem as a treatment of 'another famous homecoming', one of several misrepresentations of his work by the first Swedish translator of *The Lord of the Rings*.

Mis-readings like the one alluded to above are not uncommon where *The Homecoming* is concerned; the text has for many years maintained something of a reputation as an obscurity in the Tolkien canon. We might say that the precedent was set from the start. Its first publication came in a 1953 volume of the academic journal *Essays and Studies* – despite the fact that *The Homecoming* is, at its titular heart, a play in alliterative verse. Its awkward fit in the journal was certainly not lost on Tolkien, who issues a kind of sheepish apology in the opening lines of 'Ofermod', the critical essay that follows his verse drama. While this scholarly endnote, which probably earned *The*

Homecoming its place in the journal, has gained considerable traction (first among scholars of *The Battle of Maldon*, and later those interested in Tolkien's own tales) the rest of the text has been, when not terribly misunderstood, largely neglected. To cite one egregious example: the stock blurb on some online booksellers for *Tree and Leaf*, the latest collection to include a reprint of *The Homecoming*, even today erroneously claims that readers will be 'treated to the translation of Tolkien's account of the *Battle of Maldon*, known as *The Homecoming of Beorhtnoth*'.

This new edition of *The Homecoming*, on the verge of the 70th anniversary of its first publication, aims to clear up such confusion and to let shine its unique poetic and scholarly qualities: as the rare completed specimen of Tolkien's mastery of alliterative verse in modern English, and the site of some of the author's most illuminating reflections on heroism, war, and poetic tradition.

To better achieve this goal, I am pleased to present here alongside *The Homecoming* two closely-related but previously unpublished works: Tolkien's prose translation of *The Battle of Maldon*, the anonymous poem which inspired the events of his verse drama, with select notes and commentary; and 'The Tradition of Versification in Old English', a wide-ranging essay on the nature of poetic and artistic tradition and *Maldon*'s place within the early English canon. For readers wishing to delve further, appendices provide additional excerpts from Tolkien's scholarly engagements with *Maldon*, an early version of *The Homecoming* in rhyming dialogue with an overview of *The Homecoming*'s creative development, and (in my own hand) a short reflection on the ways in which the text might be said to converse with the stories of Tolkien's legendarium. I hope that readers old and new will find something of interest here.

ACKNOWLEDGEMENTS

This project received plenty of help on its journey. I am grateful to Cathleen Blackburn and the Tolkien Estate for entrusting me with the work, and to Chris Smith and Sophia Schoepfer of HarperCollins for their patience and care in guiding it toward publication. For gracious assistance (in-person and remote) in accessing Tolkien's manuscripts, my sincere thanks go to Catherine McIlwaine, Tolkien Archivist at the Bodleian Library. For long and steadfast support, thanks go to Verlyn Flieger, in whose graduate seminar I first heard the voices of Tída and Totta. For generously lending his keen eyes to the interpretation of Tolkien's handwriting, thanks to Carl F. Hostetter. For much encouragement and scholarly company, thanks to Michelle Markey Butler, Chip Crane, and Eleanor Simpson. Lastly, I wish to thank my family, to whom I dedicate this book.

For Marie, Bruno, and Flavia

INTRODUCTION

POTTING *THE HOMECOMING*
OF BEORHTNOTH

The Homecoming defies easy categorization. It can be read as scholarship, alliterative verse drama, or historical fiction; it has been described as coda, epilogue, sequel, and prequel to *The Battle of Maldon* – all of which is pretty much true. Some readers may prefer to eschew or at least put off introductory discussion and come at the text fresh; but for those who require a short primer, I offer a bare summary of *The Homecoming*'s contents in the following three paragraphs.

The text comprises three parts. At its centre is a dramatic dialogue in alliterative verse (*The Homecoming* proper) that recounts the fictional journey of two of the Ealdorman (or Duke) Beorhtnoth's servants, Torhthelm (Totta) and Tídwald (Tída), sent by the Abbot of Ely to recover their lord's body on the night after a battle between English and viking forces near Maldon in 991, which is commemorated in *The Battle of Maldon*, an extant fragment of Old English verse. Totta 'is a youth, son of a

minstrel; his head is full of old lays' about the legends of
the North; Tída, on the other hand, is an old 'farmer who
had seen much fighting', though neither of the two fought
in the previous day's battle.

As this odd couple wanders through the muck and gore
of the battlefield, searching in the dark for the headless
body of Beorhtnoth, their conversation explores the tensions between youth and age, romance and realism, pagan
and Christian worldview. After much toil, and a scuffle
with desperate scavengers that leaves one more needlessly dead, the two men succeed in loading the duke's
body onto their waggon and then hit the long road to Ely
Abbey. Totta, half-asleep in the cart, has a dream vision
in which he mutters the most famous lines of the (as yet
unwritten) Old English *Maldon*, suggesting that he may
one day go on to compose that poem. His dream is interrupted by a jolt from the bumpy road, and the curtain
falls with the monks of Ely chanting the Latin Office for
the Dead. Their chant, briefly interrupted by a mysterious
voice in the dark, closes out the sombre story of Beorhtnoth's homecoming.

This dramatic-poetic core is bracketed on the front
end by 'Beorhtnoth's Death', a prefatory historical note
on the battle and its outcome; and on the back end by
'Ofermod', an essay exploring the treatment of heroism in
the Old English poem, arguing (with aplomb, and against
the grain) that the anonymous poet expresses severe criticism of Beorhtnoth's gallant blunder in allowing the much
greater viking force to cross to the mainland via a strategic
causeway and join in a 'fair' fight. These two essays were
plainly written to provide context for the verse drama and

to accommodate the academic audience of *Essays and Studies*, and they have been retained in subsequent reprints (the present volume included).

The hybrid nature of the text makes for a challenge in placing *The Homecoming* on the Tolkien bookshelf. Taken as a whole, it may be the finest demonstration of the ways Tolkien's 'scholarly studies fertilized his imagination', producing what Alan Bliss calls his 'unique blend of philological erudition and poetic imagination' ('Canute and Beorhtnoth' 335; *Finn and Hengest* preface). The verse drama itself might sit cosily alongside other examples of Tolkien's experiments in reviving the Old English alliterative metre in modern English. Some of these, like *The Fall of Arthur*, seem to share *The Homecoming*'s interest in engaging the primary world traditions and legend cycles that Tolkien loved and studied. But many noteworthy examples also find their way into his legendarium, including his massive early unfinished *Lay of the Children of Húrin* (in the *Lays of Beleriand*) as well as shorter verses like 'The Song of the Mounds of Mundburg' in *The Lord of the Rings*. Read as an imaginative coda to the Battle of Maldon – or origin story for the poem that commemorates the battle – it bears likeness to other creative 'reconstructions' like his *Sellic Spell*, the kind of fairy tale source that Tolkien supposes might lie beneath the *Beowulf* that we know. With greater emphasis on the 'Ofermod' essay, the text finds a place beside '*Beowulf*: The Monsters and the Critics' and other works of literary criticism. And, like seemingly any work of Tolkien's – scholarly or creative – published before 1954, it will inevitably be judged in part by what small light it sheds on the nature or development of *The Lord of the Rings*, undoubtedly Tolkien's masterpiece. In this sense, *The Homecoming* invites added scrutiny for its publication less than a year prior to *The Fellowship of the Ring*.

'Beorhtnoth we bear not Béowulf here', cautions Tídwald to his young companion in the verse drama, but he may well be speaking to us, too. After all, the later, shorter, mostly historical *Battle of Maldon* can hardly compare to *Beowulf*, that lodestone to Tolkien's imagination, a seemingly inexhaustible source for his scholarly speculation and creative inspiration. But *Beowulf* excepted, *The Battle of Maldon* may well have been 'the Old English poem that most influenced Tolkien's fiction' (Holmes in *The J.R.R. Tolkien Encyclopedia*). I take up the subject in the final appendix to this volume.

MANUSCRIPT AND PUBLICATION HISTORY

A substantial collection of undated manuscripts and typescripts pertaining to *The Homecoming* are held in *MS. Tolkien 5* at Oxford's Bodleian Library. Thomas Honegger, in a 2007 article for *Tolkien Studies*, labels the eleven texts in Bodleian *MS. Tolkien 5* chronologically from *A – K*, and uses the Greek α to denote the early fragment published by Christopher Tolkien in *The Treason of Isengard*. The drafts trace the work's transformation – sometimes subtle, sometimes radical – from a short rhyming dialogue (as in version *A*) to the full-blown alliterative verse drama with accompanying scholarly apparatus in the final typescript Tolkien sent away to the printers (version *K*). Other, perhaps earlier, fragments are found here and there. Christopher Tolkien describes a rough text scribbled on the back of a version of Tolkien's poem 'Errantry', and notes that a still earlier text may be found with Tolkien's artwork held in the Bodleian Library, on the verso of a pencil sketch of a countryside landscape (*TD 88*, fol. 24). The Tolkien-Gordon Archive at Leeds University also maintains an early draft of the dialogue in rhyme, which seems to slot in between the Bodleian versions *B* and *C*.

According to Christopher Tolkien, these earliest extant fragments date as far back as the early 1930s, preceding by more than twenty years the eventual publication in 1953. The stages in the text's lengthy gestation have not been dated with much clarity; Tolkien's biographer Humphrey Carpenter noted only that it was 'in existence by 1945'. The significance of this date is clarified by Christopher Tolkien's remark in the Note on the Text published with *The Lay of Aotrou and Itroun*: 'My father visited Aberystwyth as an examiner in June 1945 and left with his friend Professor Gwyn Jones several unpublished works, *Aotrou and Itroun*, *The Homecoming of Beorhtnoth*, and *Sellic Spell*'. What state *The Homecoming* had reached by 1945 remains unclear. But it would eight years later end up sharing a place with Jones's 'Language, Style, and the Anglo-Welsh' in the same volume of *Essays and Studies*.

Following its initial publication in October 1953, *The Homecoming* has since been reprinted in various anthologies, including *The Tolkien Reader* (1966), *Poems and Stories* (1980), and later editions of *Tree and Leaf*. Apart from a limited-run booklet in 1991, celebrating the 1000th anniversary of the Battle of Maldon, the present edition is the first standalone publication of *The Homecoming*.

PERFORMANCES AND RECORDING

The first footnote to the 'Ofermod' essay declares that
the verse drama was 'intended as a recitation for two
persons, two shapes in "dim shadow"', though it 'has, of
course, never been performed'. But this ceased to be true
soon after *The Homecoming*'s publication: the BBC Third
Programme produced a radio performance that was first
broadcast on 3 December 1954, and was then repeated
on 17 June of the following year. Some record of Tolkien's
correspondence with Rayner Happenstall of the BBC survives from this time – he was ultimately displeased by the
production. Tolkien actually produced his own rendering
of the drama during the build-up to this BBC performance; he 'recorded the whole thing on tape', complete
with sound effects conjured up in his study. This recording was packaged on cassette, alongside Christopher
Tolkien's reading of 'Beorhtnoth's Death' and 'Ofermod',
and gifted to attendees of the Tolkien Centenary Conference held in Oxford in 1992.

TOLKIEN'S ENGAGEMENT WITH
THE BATTLE OF MALDON

As the present volume will show, *The Homecoming* is only
a choice late fruit of Tolkien's much longer engagement
with *The Battle of Maldon*. Thus it seems appropriate to
close this introduction with a few words on what is known
about Tolkien's encounters with the poem he describes
as 'the last surviving fragment of ancient English heroic
minstrelsy'.

Such encounters certainly stretch back at least as far as his undergraduate days (1911–1915) in Exeter College, Oxford, when *The Battle of Maldon* would have been a small but inescapable part of the English curriculum – as it is today for students of Old English. Stuart Lee notes that Tolkien's personal copy of Henry Sweet's *Anglo-Saxon Reader*, inscribed and dated to the Michaelmas term of 1911, contains various marginal annotations on *The Battle of Maldon* (*'Lagustreamas'* 158). Years later, the poem naturally formed part of his repertoire as a professor, particularly during the period in which he was Rawlinson and Bosworth Professor of Anglo-Saxon (1925–1945) at Pembroke College, where his scheduled lectures on *Maldon* are recorded at least twice, in 1928 and 1930 (*Chronology* 156, 165). In 1937, Tolkien's friend and former University of Leeds colleague E.V. Gordon published what became for many years the standard edition of *Maldon*. While this was not, as in their 1925 co-edition of *Sir Gawain and the Green Knight*, an official collaboration, Gordon's preface nonetheless thanks Tolkien for his 'many corrections and contributions', and notes that Tolkien, 'with characteristic generosity, gave [him] the solution to many of the textual and philological problems discussed' in the edition (vi).

Maldon's footprint in Tolkien's published writings outside of *The Homecoming* is slight, though it is plainly not far from Tolkien's mind in the famous 1936 lecture '*Beowulf*: The Monsters and the Critics', where 'the words of Byrhtwold' (lines 312–13 of *Maldon*) are described as the 'doctrinal expression' of 'the exaltation of undefeated will' (*MC* 18). Some thirty years later, in the poem, 'For W.H.A.', part of the *Shenandoah* collection of sixtieth-birthday tributes to W.H. Auden, Tolkien recalled his friend's legendary namesake: 'Wighelm's son who in war was slain / at Byrhtnoth's side by the Blackwater / in the famous defeat'. Yet these scant and scattered allusions belie the remarkable breadth and depth of Tolkien's interest in *Maldon* which even a cursory glance at Tolkien's academic papers in the Bodleian Library shows. Published here for the first time is a taste of this long and fruitful engagement.

A final word on my arrangement: though presented first in this volume, *The Homecoming* is clearly the latest of the texts assembled here. The reader may fairly ask why *Maldon*, as the inspiration for *The Homecoming*, does not open the volume. While this placement may on the one hand acknowledge *The Homecoming*'s broader appeal and status as a remarkable culmination of much that Tolkien thought and felt about *Maldon*, it also implicitly emphasizes Tolkien's abiding interest in poetic craft and in the process of literary sub-creation. For in placing the journey of Tída and Totta before *The Battle of Maldon*, this edition follows the internal chronology of Tolkien's fictional investigation: it is only after the action of *The Homecoming* that the famous Old English poem can be made.

PART ONE

The Homecoming of Beorhtnoth Beorhthelm's Son

(I)

BEORHTNOTH'S DEATH

In August of the year 991, in the reign of Æthelred II, a battle was fought near Maldon in Essex. On the one side was the defence-force of Essex, on the other a viking host that had ravaged Ipswich. The English were commanded by Beorhtnoth son of Beorhthelm, the duke of Essex, a man renowned in his day: powerful, fearless, proud. He was now old and hoar, but vigorous and valiant, and his white head towered high above other men, for he was exceedingly tall.* The 'Danes' – they were on this occasion probably for the most part Norwegians – were, according to one version of the Anglo-Saxon Chronicle, led by Anlaf, famous in Norse saga and history as Olaf Tryggvason, later to become King of Norway.† The Northmen had sailed up the estuary of the Pante, now called the Blackwater, and encamped on Northey Island. The Northmen

---

* According to one estimate 6 foot 9 inches tall. This estimate was based on the length and size of his bones when examined, in his tomb at Ely, in A.D. 1769.
† That Olaf Tryggvason was actually present at Maldon is now thought to be doubtful. But his name was known to Englishmen. He had been in Britain before, and was certainly here again in 994.

and the English were thus separated by an arm of the river; filled by the incoming tide, it could only be crossed by a 'bridge' or causeway, difficult to force in the face of a determined defence.* The defence was resolute. But the vikings knew, or so it would seem, what manner of a man they had to deal with: they asked for leave to cross the ford, so that a fair fight could be joined. Beorhtnoth accepted the challenge and allowed them to cross. This act of pride and misplaced chivalry proved fatal. Beorhtnoth was slain and the English routed; but the duke's 'household', his *heorðwerod*, containing the picked knights and officers of his bodyguard, some of them members of his own family, fought on, until they all fell dead beside their lord.

A fragment – a large fragment, 325 lines long – of a contemporary poem has been preserved: it has no end and no beginning, and no title, but is now generally known as *The Battle of Maldon*. It tells of the demand of the vikings for tribute in return for peace; of Beorhtnoth's proud refusal, and challenge, and the defence of the 'bridge'; the cunning request of the vikings, and the crossing of the causeway; the last fight of Beorhtnoth, the falling of his golden-hilted sword from his maimed hand, and the hewing of his body by the heathen men. The end of the fragment, almost half of it, tells of the last stand of the bodyguard. The names, deeds, and speeches of many of the Englishmen are recorded.

The duke Beorhtnoth was a defender of the monks, and

---

* According to the views of E.D. Laborde, now generally accepted. The causeway or 'hard' between Northey and the mainland is still there.

a patron of the church, especially of the abbey of Ely. After the battle the Abbot of Ely obtained his body and buried it in the abbey. His head had been hacked off and was not recovered; it was replaced in the tomb by a ball of wax.

According to the late, and largely unhistorical, account in the twelfth-century *Liber Eliensis*, the Abbot of Ely went himself with some of his monks to the battlefield. But in the following poem it is supposed that the abbot and his monks came only as far as Maldon, and that they there remained, sending two men, servants of the duke, to the battlefield some distance away, late in the day after the battle. They took a waggon, and were to bring back Beorhtnoth's body. They left the waggon near the end of the causeway and began to search among the slain: very many had fallen on both sides. Torhthelm (colloquially Totta) is a youth, son of a minstrel; his head is full of old lays concerning the heroes of northern antiquity, such as Finn, king of Frisia; Fróda of the Hathobards; Béowulf; and Hengest and Horsa, traditional leaders of the English Vikings in the days of Vortigern (called by the English Wyrtgeorn). Tídwald (in short Tída) was an old *ceorl*, a farmer who had seen much fighting in the English defence-levies. Neither of these men were actually in the battle. After leaving the waggon they became separated in the gathering dusk. Night falls, dark and clouded. Torhthelm is found alone in a part of the field where the dead lie thick.

From the old poem are derived the proud words of Offa at a council before the battle, and the name of the gallant young Ælfwine (scion of an ancient noble house in Mercia) whose courage was commended by Offa. There also are found the names of the two Wulfmærs: Wulfmær, son of Beorhtnoth's sister; and Wulfmær the young, son of Wulfstan, who together with Ælfnoth fell grievously hewn beside Beorhtnoth. Near the end of the surviving fragment an old retainer, Beorhtwold, as he prepares to die in the last desperate stand, utters the famous words, a summing up of the heroic code, that are here spoken in a dream by Torhthelm:

Hige sceal þe heardra, heorte þe cenre,
mod sceal þe mare þe ure mægen lytlað.

'Will shall be the sterner, heart the bolder, spirit the greater as our strength lessens'.

It is here implied, as is indeed probable, that these words were not 'original', but an ancient and honoured expression of heroic will; Beorhtwold is all the more, not the less, likely for that reason actually to have used them in his last hour.

The third English voice in the dark, speaking after the *Dirige* is first heard, uses rhyme: presaging the fading end of the old heroic alliterative measure. The old poem is composed in a free form of the alliterative line, the last surviving fragment of ancient English heroic minstrelsy. In that measure, little if at all freer (though used for dialogue) than the verse of *The Battle of Maldon*, the present modern poem is written.

The rhyming lines are an echo of some verses, preserved in the *Historia Eliensis*, referring to King Canute:

(I) BEORHTNOTH'S DEATH

Merie sungen ðe muneches binnen Ely,
ða Cnut ching reu ðerby.
'Roweð, cnites, noer the land
And here we ther muneches saeng'.

(II)

THE HOMECOMING OF
BEORHTNOTH BEORHTHELM'S SON

*The sound is heard of a man moving uncertainly and
breathing noisily in the darkness. Suddenly a voice speaks,
loudly and sharply.*

TORHTHELM

Halt! What do you want? Hell take you! Speak!

TÍDWALD

Totta! I know you by your teeth rattling.

TORHTHELM

Why, Tída, you! The time seemed long
alone among the lost. They lie so queer.
I've watched and waited, till the wind sighing
was like words whispered by waking ghosts
that in my ears muttered.

TÍDWALD

          And your eyes fancied
barrow-wights and bogies. It's a black darkness
since the moon foundered; but mark my words:

8

not far from here we'll find the master,
by all accounts.

Tidwald lets out a faint beam from a dark-lantern. An owl hoots.
A dark shape flits through the beam of light. Torhthelm starts back
and overturns the lantern, which Tida had set on the ground.

What ails you now?

TORHTHELM
Lord save us! Listen!

TÍDWALD
My lad, you're crazed.
your fancies and your fears make foes of nothing.
Help me to heave 'em! It's heavy labour
to lug them alone: long ones and short ones,
the thick and the thin. Think less, and talk less
of ghosts Forget your gleeman's stuff!
Their ghosts are under ground, or else God has them;
and wolves don't walk as in Woden's days,
not here in Essex. If any there be,
they'll be two-leggéd. There, turn him over!

An owl hoots again.

It's only an owl.

TORHTHELM
An ill boding.
Owls are omens. But I'm not afraid,
not of fancied fears. A fool call me,
but more men than I find the mirk gruesome
among the dead unshrouded. It's like the dim shadow

9

of heathen hell, in the hopeless kingdom
where search is vain. We might seek for ever
and yet miss the master in this mirk, Tída.
    O lord beloved, where do you lie tonight,
your head so hoar upon a hard pillow,
and your limbs lying in long slumber?

Tídwald lets out again the light of the dark-lantern.

TÍDWALD

Look here, my lad, where they lie thickest!
Here! lend a hand! This head we know!
Wulfmær it is. I'll wager aught
not far did he fall from friend and master.

TORHTHELM

His sister-son! The songs tell us,
ever near shall be at need nephew to uncle.

TÍDWALD

Nay, he's not here – or he's hewn out of ken.
It was the other I meant, th' Eastsaxon lad,
Wulfstan's youngster. It's a wicked business
to gather them ungrown. A gallant boy, too,
and the makings of a man.

TORHTHELM

            Have mercy on us!
He was younger than I, by a year or more.

TÍDWALD

Here's Ælfnoth, too, by his arm lying.

TORHTHELM

As he would have wished it. In work or play
they were fast fellows, and faithful to their lord,
as close to him as kin.

TÍDWALD

Curse this lamplight
and my eyes' dimness! My oath I'll take
they fell in his defence, and not far away
now master lies. Move them gently!

TORHTHELM

Brave lads! But it's bad when bearded men
put shield at back and shun battle,
running like roe-deer, while the red heathen
beat down their boys. May the blast of Heaven
light on the dastards that to death left them
to England's shame! And here's Ælfwine:
barely bearded, and his battle's over.

TÍDWALD

That's bad, Totta. He was a brave lordling,
and we need his like: a new weapon
of the old metal. As eager as fire,
and as staunch as steel. Stern-tongued at times,
and outspoken after Offa's sort.

TORHTHELM

Offa! he's silenced. Not all liked him;
many would have muzzled him, had master let them.
'There are cravens at council that crow proudly
with the hearts of hens': so I hear he said
at the lords' meeting. As lays remind us:

'What at the mead man vows, when morning comes
let him with deeds answer, or his drink vomit
and a sot be shown'. But the songs wither,
and the world worsens. I wish I'd been here,
not left with the luggage and the lazy thralls,
cooks and sutlers! By the Cross, Tída,
I loved him no less than any lord with him;
and a poor freeman may prove in the end
more tough when tested than titled earls
who count back their kin to kings ere Woden.

TÍDWALD

You can talk, Totta! Your time'll come,
and it'll look less easy than lays make it.
Bitter taste has iron, and the bite of swords
is cruel and cold, when you come to it.
Then God guard you, if your glees falter!
When your shield is shivered, between shame and death
is hard choosing. Help me with this one!
There, heave him over – the hound's carcase,
Hulking heathen!

TORHTHELM

                    Hide it, Tída!
Put the lantern out! He's looking at me.
I can't abide his eyes, bleak and evil
as Grendel's in the moon.

TÍDWALD

                    Ay, he's a grim fellow,
but he's dead and done-for. Danes don't trouble me

save with swords and axes. They can smile or glare,
once hell has them. Come, haul the next!

TORHTHELM

Look! Here's a limb! A long yard, and thick
as three men's thighs.

TÍDWALD

I thought as much.
Now bow your head, and hold your babble
for a moment Totta! It's the master at last.

There is silence for a short while.

Well, here he is – or what Heaven's left us:
the longest legs in the land, I guess.

TORHTHELM (*His voice rises to a chant.*)

His head was higher than the helm of kings
with heathen crowns, his heart keener
and his soul clearer than swords of heroes
polished and proven; than plated gold
his worth was greater. From the world has passed
a prince peerless in peace and war,
just in judgement, generous-handed
as the golden lords of long ago.
He has gone to God glory seeking,
Beorhtnoth beloved.

TÍDWALD

Brave words, my lad!
The woven staves have yet worth in them
for woeful hearts. But there's work to do,
ere the funeral begins.

TORHTHELM

                I've found it, Tída!
Here's his sword lying! I could swear to it
by the golden hilts.

TÍDWALD

                I'm glad to hear it.
How it was missed is a marvel. He is marred cruelly.
Few tokens else shall we find on him;
they've left us little of the lord we knew.

TORHTHELM

Ah, woe and worse! The wolvish heathens
have hewn off his head, and the hulk left us
mangled with axes. What a murder it is,
this bloody fighting!

TÍDWALD

               Aye, that's battle for you,
and no worse today than wars you sing of,
when Fróda fell, and Finn was slain.
The world wept then, as it weeps today:
you can hear the tears through the harp's twanging.
Come, bend your back! We must bear away
the cold leavings. Catch hold of the legs!
Now lift – gently! Now lift again!

They shuffle along slowly.

TORHTHELM

Dear still shall be this dead body,
though men have marred it.

Torhthelm's voice rises again to a chant.

Now mourn for ever
Saxon and English, from the sea's margin
to the western forest! The wall is fallen,
women are weeping; the wood is blazing
and the fire flaming as a far beacon.
Build high the barrow his bones to keep!
For here shall be hid both helm and sword;
and to the ground be given golden corslet,
and rich raiment and rings gleaming,
wealth unbegrudged for the well-beloved;
of the friends of men first and noblest,
to his hearth-comrades help unfailing,
to his folk the fairest father of peoples.
Glory loved he; now glory earning
his grave shall be green, while ground or sea,
while word or woe in the world lasteth.

TÍDWALD

Good words enough, gleeman Totta!
You laboured long as you lay, I guess,
in the watches of the night, while the wise slumbered.
But I'd rather have rest, and my rueful thoughts.
These are Christian days, though the cross is heavy;
Beorhtnoth we bear not Béowulf here:
no pyres for him, nor piling of mounds;
and the gold will be given to the good abbot.
Let the monks mourn him and mass be chanted!
With learned Latin they'll lead him home,
if we can bring him back. The body's weighty!

15

TORHTHELM

Dead men drag earthward. Now down a spell!
My back's broken, and the breath has left me.

TÍDWALD

If you spent less in speech, you would speed better.
But the cart's not far, so keep at it!
Now start again, and in step with me!
A steady pace does it.

Torhthelm halts suddenly.

You stumbling dolt,
Look where you're going!

TORHTHELM

For the Lord's pity,
Halt, Tída, here! Hark now, and look!

TÍDWALD

Look where, my lad?

TORHTHELM

To the left yonder.
There's a shade creeping, a shadow darker
than the western sky, there walking crouched!
Two now together! Troll-shapes, I guess,
or hell-walkers. They've a halting gait,
groping groundwards with grisly arms.

TÍDWALD

Nameless nightshades – naught else can I see,
till they walk nearer. You're witch-sighted
to tell fiends from men in this foul darkness.

TORHTHELM

Then listen, Tída! There are low voices,
moans and muttering, and mumbled laughter.
They are moving hither!

TÍDWALD

Yes, I mark it now,
I can hear something.

TORHTHELM

Hide the lantern!

TÍDWALD

Lay down the body and lie by it!
Now stone-silent! There are steps coming.

*They crouch on the ground. The sound of stealthy steps grows
louder and nearer. When they are close at hand Tidwald suddenly
shouts out:*

Hullo there, my lads! You're late comers,
if it's fighting you look for; but I can find you some,
if you need it tonight. You'll get nothing cheaper.

*There is a noise of scuffling in the dark. Then there is a shriek.
Torhthelm's voice rings out shrill.*

TORHTHELM

You snuffling swine, I'll slit you for it!
Take your trove then! Ho! Tída there!
I've slain this one. He'll slink no more.
If swords he was seeking, he soon found one,
by the biting end.

TÍDWALD

My bogey-slayer!
Bold heart would you borrow with Beorhtnoth's sword?
Nay, wipe it clean! And keep your wits!
That blade was made for better uses.
You wanted no weapon: a wallop on the nose,
or a boot behind, and the battle's over
with the likes of these. Their life's wretched,
but why kill the creatures, or crow about it?
There are dead enough around. Were he a Dane, mind you,
I'd let you boast – and there's lots abroad
not far away, the filthy thieves:
I hate 'em, by my heart, heathen or sprinkled,
the Devil's offspring.

TORHTHELM

The Danes, you say!
Make haste! Let's go! I'd half forgotten.
There may be more at hand our murder plotting.
We'll have the pirate pack come pouring on us,
if they hear us brawling.

TÍDWALD

My brave swordsman!
These weren't Northmen! Why should Northmen come?
They've had their fill of hewing and fighting,
and picked their plunder: the place is bare.
They're in Ipswich now with the ale running,
or lying off London in their long vessels,
while they drink to Thor and drown the sorrow
of hell's children. These are hungry folk

and masterless men, miserable skulkers.
They're corpse-strippers: a cursèd game
and shame to think of. What are you shuddering at?

TORHTHELM

Come on now quick! Christ forgive me,
and these evil days, when unregretted
men lie mouldering, and the manner of wolves
the folk follow in fear and hunger,
their dead unpitying to drag and plunder!
Look there yonder! There's a lean shadow,
a third of the thieves. Let's thrash the villain!

TÍDWALD

Nay, let him alone! Or we'll lose the way.
As it is we've wandered, and I'm bewildered enough.
He won't try attacking two men by himself.
Lift your end there! Lift up, I say.
Put your foot forward.

TORHTHELM

                  Can you find it, Tída?
I haven't a notion now in these nightshadows
where we left the waggon. I wish we were back!

They shuffle along without speaking for a while.

Walk wary, man! There's water by us;
you'll blunder over the brink. Here's the Blackwater!
Another step that way, and in the stream we'd be
like fools floundering – and the flood's running.

TÍDWALD

We've come to the causeway. The cart's near it,
so courage, my boy. If we can carry him on
few steps further, the first stage is passed.

They move a few paces more.

By Edmund's head! though his own's missing,
our lord's not light. Now lay him down!
Here's the waggon waiting. I wish we could drink
his funeral ale without further trouble
on the bank right here. The beer he gave
was good and plenty to gladden your heart,
both strong and brown. I'm in a stew of sweat.
Let's stay a moment.

TORHTHELM

(*After a pause.*) It's strange to me
how they came across this causeway here,
or forced a passage without fierce battle;
but there are few tokens to tell of fighting.
A hill of heathens one would hope to find,
but none lie near.

TÍDWALD

No, more's the pity.
Alas, my friend, our lord was at fault,
or so in Maldon this morning men were saying.
Too proud, too princely! But his pride's cheated,
and his princedom has passed, so we'll praise his valour.
He let them cross the causeway, so keen was he
to give minstrels matter for mighty songs.
Needlessly noble. It should never have been:

bidding bows be still, and the bridge opening,
matching more with few in mad handstrokes!
Well, doom he dared, and died for it.

TORHTHELM

So the last is fallen of the line of earls,
from Saxon lords long-descended
who sailed the seas, as songs tell us,
from Angel in the East, with eager swords
upon war's anvil the Welsh smiting.
Realms here they won and royal kingdoms,
and in olden days this isle conquered.
And now from the North need comes again:
wild blows the wind of war to Britain!

TÍDWALD

And in the neck we catch it, and are nipped as chill
as poor men were then. Let the poets babble,
but perish all pirates! When the poor are robbed
and lose the land they loved and toiled on,
they must die and dung it. No dirge for them,
and their wives and children work in serfdom.

TORHTHELM

But Æthelred'll prove less easy prey
than Wyrtgeorn was; and I'll wager, too,
this Anlaf of Norway will never equal
Hengest or Horsa!

TÍDWALD

                              We'll hope not, lad!
Come, lend your hand to the lifting again,
then your task is done. There, turn him round!

Hold the shanks now, while I heave the shoulders.
Now, up your end! Up! That's finished.
There cover him with the cloth.

TORHTHELM

               It should be clean linen
not a dirty blanket.

TÍDWALD

               It must do for now.
The monks are waiting in Maldon for us,
and the abbot with them. We're hours behind.
Get up now and in! Your eyes can weep,
or your mouth can pray. I'll mind the horses.
Gee up, boys, then. (*He cracks a whip.*) Gee up, and away!

TORHTHELM

God guide our road to a good ending!

> *There is a pause, in which a rumbling and a creaking*
> *of wheels is heard.*

How these wheels do whine! They'll hear the creak
for miles away over mire and stone.

> *A longer pause in which no word is spoken.*

Where first do we make for? Have we far to go?
The night is passing, and I'm near finished...
Say, Tída, Tída! Is your tongue stricken?

TÍDWALD

I'm tired of talk. My tongue's resting.
'Where first' you say? A fool's question!
To Maldon and the monks, and then miles onward

to Ely and the abbey. It'll end sometime;
but the roads are bad in these ruinous days.
No rest for you yet! Were you reckoning on bed?
The best you'll get is the bottom of the cart
with his body for bolster.

TORHTHELM

>You're a brute, Tída.

TÍDWALD

It's only plain language. If a poet sang you:
'I bowed my head on his breast beloved,
and weary of weeping woeful slept I;
thus joined we journeyed, gentle master
and faithful servant, over fen and boulder
to his last resting and love's ending',
you'd not call it cruel. I have cares of my own
in my heart, Totta, and my head's weary.
I am sorry for you, and for myself also.
Sleep, lad, then! Sleep! The slain won't trouble,
if your head be heavy, or the wheels grumble.

>*He speaks to the horses.*

Gee up, my boys! And on you go!
There's food ahead and fair stables,
for the monks are kind. Put the miles behind.

*The creaking and rattling of the waggon, and the sound of hoofs,
continue for some time, during which no words are spoken. After
a while lights glimmer in the distance. Torhthelm speaks from the
waggon, drowsily and half dreaming.*

23

TORHTHELM

There are candles in the dark and cold voices.
I hear mass chanted for master's soul
in Ely isle. Thus ages pass,
and men after men. Mourning voices
of women weeping. So the world passes;
day follows day, and the dust gathers,
his tomb crumbles, as time gnaws it,
and his kith and kindred out of ken dwindle.
So men flicker and in the mirk go out.
The world withers and the wind rises;
the candles are quenched. Cold falls the night.

> *The lights disappear as he speaks. Torhthelm's voice becomes*
> *louder, but it is still the voice of one speaking in a dream.*

It's dark! It's dark, and doom coming!
Is no light left us? A light kindle,
and fan the flame! Lo! Fire now wakens,
hearth is burning, house is lighted,
men there gather. Out of the mists they come
through darkling doors whereat doom waiteth.
Hark! I hear them in the hall chanting:
stern words they sing with strong voices.
(*He chants.*) Heart shall be bolder, harder be purpose,
more proud the spirit as our power lessens!
Mind shall not falter nor mood waver,
though doom shall come and dark conquer.

> *There is a great bump and jolt of the cart.*

Hey! What a bump, Tída! My bones are shaken,
and my dream shattered. It's dark and cold.

TÍDWALD

Aye, a bump on the bone is bad for dreams,
and it's cold waking. But your words were queer,
Torhthelm my lad, with your talk of wind
and doom conquering and a dark ending.
It sounded fey and fell-hearted,
and heathenish, too: I don't hold with that.
It's night right enough; but there's no firelight:
dark is over all, and dead is master.
When morning comes, it'll be much like others:
more labour and loss till the land's ruined;
ever work and war till the world passes.

The cart rumbles and bumps on.

Hey! rattle and bump over rut and boulder!
The roads are rough and rest is short
for English men in Æthelred's day.

*The rumbling of the cart dies away. There is complete silence
for a while. Slowly the sound of voices chanting begins to
be heard. Soon the words, though faint, can
be distinguished.*

Dirige, Domine, in conspectu tuo viam meam.
Introibo in domum tuam: adorabo ad templum
sanctum tuum in timore tuo.

(A Voice in the dark):

Sadly they sing, the monks of Ely isle!
Row men, row! Let us listen here a while!

The chanting becomes loud and clear. Monks bearing a bier amid tapers pass across the scene.

Dirige, Domine, in conspectu tuo viam meam.
Introibo in domum tuam: adorabo ad templum sanctum tuum in timore tuo.
Domine, deduc me in iustitia tua: propter inimicos meos dirige in conspectu tuo viam meam.
Gloria Patri et Filio et Spiritui Sancto: sicut erat in principio et nunc et semper et in saecula saeculorum.
Dirige, Domine, in conspectu tuo viam meam.

They pass, and the chanting fades into silence.

(III)

OFERMOD

This piece, somewhat larger than the Old English fragment that inspired it, was composed primarily as verse, to
be condemned or approved as such.* But to merit a place
in *Essays and Studies* it must, I suppose, contain at least by
implication criticism of the matter and manner of the Old
English poem (or of its critics).

From that point of view it may be said to be an
extended comment on lines 89, 90 of the original: *ða se
eorl ongan for his ofermode alyfan landes to fela laþere ðeode*,
'then the earl in his overmastering pride actually yielded
ground to the enemy, as he should not have done'. *The
Battle of Maldon* has usually been regarded rather as an
extended comment on, or illustration of the words of the
old retainer Beorhtwold, 312, 313, cited above, and used
in the present piece. They are the best-known lines of the
poem, possibly of all Old English verse. Yet except in the
excellence of their expression, they seem to me of less

---

* It was indeed plainly intended as a recitation for two persons, two
shapes in 'dim shadow', with the help of a few gleams of light and
appropriate noises and a chant at the end. It has, of course, never
been performed.

interest than the earlier lines; at any rate the full force of the poem is missed unless the two passages are considered together.

The words of Beorhtwold have been held to be the finest expression of the northern heroic spirit, Norse or English; the clearest statement of the doctrine of uttermost endurance in the service of indomitable will. The poem as a whole has been called 'the only purely heroic poem extant in Old English'. Yet the doctrine appears in this clarity, and (approximate) purity, precisely because it is put in the mouth of a subordinate, a man for whom the object of his will was decided by another, who had no responsibility downwards, only loyalty upwards. Personal pride was therefore in him at its lowest, and love and loyalty at their highest.

For this 'northern heroic spirit' is never quite pure; it is of gold and an alloy. Unalloyed it would direct a man to endure even death unflinching, when necessary: that is when death may help the achievement of some object of will, or when life can only be purchased by denial of what one stands for. But since such conduct is held admirable, the alloy of personal good name was never wholly absent. Thus Leofsunu in *The Battle of Maldon* holds himself to his loyalty by the fear of reproach if he returns home alive. This motive may, of course, hardly go beyond 'conscience': self-judgement in the light of the opinion of his peers, to which the 'hero' himself wholly assents; he would act the same, if there were no witnesses.* Yet this element of pride, in the form of the desire for honour and

---

* Cf. *Sir Gawain and the Green Knight*, 2127–31.

glory, in life and after death, tends to grow, to become a chief motive, driving a man beyond the bleak heroic necessity to excess – to chivalry. 'Excess' certainly, even if it be approved by contemporary opinion, when it not only goes beyond need and duty, but interferes with it.

Thus Beowulf (according to the motives ascribed to him by the student of heroic-chivalric character who wrote the poem about him) does more than he need, eschewing weapons in order to make his struggle with Grendel a 'sporting' fight: which will enhance his personal glory; though it will put him in unnecessary peril, and weaken his chances of ridding the Danes of an intolerable affliction. But Beowulf has no duty to the Danes, he is still a subordinate with no responsibilities downwards; and his glory is also the honour of his side, of the Geatas; above all, as he himself says, it will redound to the credit of the lord of his allegiance, Hygelac. Yet he does not rid himself of his chivalry, the excess persists, even when he is an old king upon whom all the hopes of a people rest. He will not deign to lead a force against the dragon, as wisdom might direct even a hero to do; for, as he explains in a long 'vaunt', his many victories have relieved him of fear. He will only use a sword on this occasion, since wrestling singlehanded with a dragon is too hopeless even for the chivalric spirit. But he dismisses his twelve companions. He is saved from defeat, and the essential object, destruction of the dragon, only achieved by the loyalty of a subordinate. Beowulf's chivalry would otherwise have ended in his own useless death, with the dragon still at large. As it is, a subordinate is placed in greater peril than he need have been, and though he does not pay the penalty of his master's *mod* with his own life, the people lose their king disastrously.

In *Beowulf* we have only a legend of 'excess' in a chief. The case of Beorhtnoth is still more pointed even as a story: but it is also drawn from real life by a contemporary author. Here we have Hygelac behaving like young Beowulf: making a 'sporting fight' on level terms; but at other people's expense. In his situation he was not a subordinate, but the authority to be obeyed on the spot; and he was responsible for all the men under him, not to throw away their lives except with one object, the defence of the realm from an implacable foe. He says himself that it is his purpose to defend the realm of Æthelred, the people, and the land (52–3). It was heroic for him and his men to fight, to annihilation if necessary, in the attempt to destroy or hold off the invaders. It was wholly unfitting that he should treat a desperate battle with this sole real object as a sporting match, to the ruin of his purpose and duty.

Why did Beorhtnoth do this? Owing to a defect of character, no doubt; but a character, we may surmise, not only formed by nature, but moulded also by 'aristocratic tradition', enshrined in tales and verse of poets now lost save for echoes. Beorhtnoth was chivalrous rather than strictly heroic. Honour was in itself a motive, and he sought it at the risk of placing his *heorðwerod*, all the men most dear to him, in a truly heroic situation, which they could redeem only by death. Magnificent perhaps, but certainly wrong. Too foolish to be heroic. And the folly Beorhtnoth at any rate could not wholly redeem by death.

This was recognized by the poet of *The Battle of Maldon*, though the lines in which his opinion are expressed are little regarded, or played down. The translation of them given above is (I believe) accurate in representing the force and implication of his words, though most will be more familiar with Ker's: 'then the earl of his overboldness granted ground too much to the hateful people'.* They are lines in fact of *severe* criticism, though not incompatible with loyalty, and even love. Songs of praise at Beorhtnoth's funeral may well have been made of him, not unlike the lament of the twelve princes for Beowulf; but they too may have ended on the ominous note struck by the last word of the greater poem: *lofgeornost* 'most desirous of glory'.

So far as the fragment of his work goes, the poet of *Maldon* did not elaborate the point contained in lines 89–90; though if the poem had any rounded ending and final appraisement (as is likely, for it is certainly not a work of hot haste), it was probably resumed. Yet if he felt moved to criticize and express disapproval at all, then his study of the behaviour of the *heorðwerod*, lacks the sharpness and tragic quality that he intended, if his criticism is

---

* *To fela* means in Old English idiom that no ground at all should have been conceded. And *ofermod* does not mean 'overboldness', not even if we give full value to the *ofer*, remembering how strongly the taste and wisdom of the English (whatever their actions) rejected 'excess'. *Wita scal geþyldig...ne næfre gielpes to georn, ær he geare cunne.* But *mod*, though it may contain or imply courage, does not mean 'boldness' any more than Middle English *corage*. It means 'spirit', or when unqualified 'high spirit', of which the most usual manifestation is pride. But in *ofer-mod* it is qualified, with disapproval: *ofermod* is in fact always a word of condemnation. In verse the noun occurs only twice, once applied to Beorhtnoth, and once to Lucifer.

not fully valued. By it the loyalty of the retinue is greatly enhanced. Their part was to endure and die, and not to question, though a recording poet may fairly comment that someone had blundered. In their situation heroism was superb. Their duty was unimpaired by the error of their master, and (more poignantly) neither in the hearts of those near to the old man was love lessened. It is the heroism of obedience and love not of pride or wilfuness that is the most heroic and the most moving; from Wiglaf under his kinsman's shield, to Beorhtwold at Maldon, down to Balaclava, even if it is enshrined in verse no better than *The Charge of the Light Brigade*.

Beorhtnoth was wrong, and he died for his folly. But it was a noble error, or the error of a noble. It was not for his *heorðwerod* to blame him; probably many would not have felt him blameworthy, being themselves noble and chivalrous. But poets, as such, are above chivalry, or even heroism; and if they give any depth to their treatment of such themes, then, even in spite of themselves, these 'moods' and the objects to which they are directed will be questioned.

We have two poets that study at length the heroic and chivalrous with both art and thought in the older ages: one near the beginning in *Beowulf*; one near the end in *Sir Gawain*. And probably a third, more near the middle, in *Maldon*, if we had all his work. It is not surprising that any consideration of the work of one of these leads to the others. *Sir Gawain*, the latest, is the most fully conscious, and is in plain intention a criticism or valuation of a whole code of sentiment and conduct, in which heroic courage is only a part, with different loyalties to serve.

Yet it is a poem with many inner likenesses to *Beowulf*, deeper than the use of the old 'alliterative'* metre, which is nonetheless significant. Sir Gawain, as the exemplar of chivalry, is of course shown to be deeply concerned for his own honour, and though the things considered honourable may have shifted or been enlarged, loyalty to word and to allegiance, and unflinching courage remain. These are tested in adventures no nearer to ordinary life than Grendel or the dragon; but Gawain's conduct is made more worthy, and more worth considering, again because he is a subordinate. He is involved in peril and the certain prospect of death simply by loyalty, and the desire to secure the safety and dignity of his lord, King Arthur. And upon him depends in his quest the honour of his lord and of his *heorðwerod*, the Round Table. It is no accident that in this poem, as in *Maldon* and in *Beowulf*, we have criticism of the lord, of the owner of the allegiance. The words are striking, though less so than the small part they have played in criticism of the poem (as also in *Maldon*). Yet thus spoke the court of the great King Arthur, when Sir Gawain rode away:

> *Before God 'tis a shame*
> *that thou, lord, must be lost, who art in life so noble!*
> *To meet his match among men, Marry, 'tis not easy!*
> *To behave with more heed would have behoved one of sense,*
> *and that dear lord duly a duke to have made,*
> *illustrious leader of liegemen in this land as befits him;*

---

* It is probably the first work to apply the word 'letters' to this metre, which has in fact never regarded them.

33

and that better would have been than to be butchered to death,
beheaded by an elvish man for an arrogant vaunt.
Who ever heard tell of a king such courses taking,
as knights quibbling at court at their Christmas games!

Beowulf is a rich poem: there are of course many other
sides to the description of the manner of the hero's death;
and the consideration (sketched above) of the changing
values of chivalry in youth and in age and responsibility
is only an ingredient. Yet it is plainly there and though
the author's main imagination was moving in wider
ways, criticism of the lord and owner of the allegiance is
touched on.

Thus the lord may indeed receive credit from the
deeds of his knights, but he must not use their loyalty or
imperil them simply for that purpose. It was not Hygelac
that sent Beowulf to Denmark through any boast or rash
vow. His words to Beowulf on his return are no doubt
an alteration of the older story (which peeps rather
through in the egging of the *snotere ceorlas*, 202–4); but
they are the more significant for that. We hear, 1992–7,
that Hygelac had tried to restrain Beowulf from a rash
adventure. Very properly. But at the end the situation is
reversed. We learn, 3076–83, that Wiglaf and the Geatas
regarded any attack on the dragon as rash, and had
tried to restrain the king from the perilous enterprise,
with words very like those used by Hygelac long before.
But the king wished for glory, or for a glorious death,
and courted disaster. There could be no more pungent
criticism in a few words of 'chivalry' in one of responsibility than Wiglaf's exclamation: *oft sceall eorl monig anes*

willan wræc adreogan, 'by one man's will many must woe endure'. These words the poet of *Maldon* might have inscribed at the head of his work.

NOTES

(I)
BEORHTNOTH'S DEATH

Æthelred II

King from 978–1013 and again from 1014 to his death in 1016. His reign was marred by many viking invasions. In draft material, Tolkien notes that 'trying to buy off the Danes with *gafol* (tribute) was first adopted' as English policy following the disaster at Maldon. And he more than once refers to Æthelred's disparaging epithet, 'the Unready'.

Beorhtnoth

On Tolkien's unusual spelling of the *Maldon* hero's name, Michael D.C. Drout notes:

> The manuscript reading of the name is 'Byrhtnoth'. Tolkien emended the 'y' to the diphthong 'eo' ... indicating his understanding of the poet's likely pronunciation of the name in the Eastern dialect in which most scholars believe it was written. The poem as we have it is in West Saxon' (161).

This is corroborated by Tolkien's own words on the matter. Among his linguistic notes on *Maldon*, he describes the shift 'Byrhtnoð for *Beorht' as 'a Late West Saxon change' (*MS. Tolkien A 30/2*, fol. 165). And, in abandoned material for the scholarly portions of *The Homecoming*, he draws attention to the space of time that probably lies between oral composition and written record: the *Maldon* manuscript, 'now destroyed by fire, was probably almost a century later than the composition of the poem' (*MS. Tolkien 5*, fol. 88). As his drama is set just a day after the battle, and his interest is partly in recovering the poem's origins, Tolkien opts for the older spelling.

led by Anlaf...

None of the viking enemies are identified by name in the poem. Throughout Part I of *The Homecoming*, Tolkien acknowledges the 'soup of story' that shapes our understanding of the battle – the inconsistent Anglo-Saxon Chronicle, 'the late, and largely unhistorical' *Liber Eliensis* – even as he prepares to add to it with his own verse drama. Further speculation as to the identity of the invaders emerges in draft material: 'The viking-leaders were probably called *Jósteinn* and *Guðmundr*' (*MS. Tolkien 5*, fol. 62v).

misplaced chivalry

Chivalry, an anachronistic term derived from Old French, emerges as a key term in Tolkien's work on *Maldon*. It is taken up at length in the 'Ofermod' essay, and it is, tellingly, part of Tolkien's gloss for *ofermod* ('overconfident chivalry') in his prose translation of the OE poem. Tolkien probably found its connections to reputation and to the courtly 'game' of honour apt. As an anachronism it echoes Tolkien's interest in changing times and attitudes; the jarring word choice may perhaps emphasize something of Beorhtnoth's misjudgment in the misplacement of his men, and of *The Homecoming*'s wider interest in changing heroic tradition over time.

abbey of Ely

The family's patronage of Ely Abbey continued after

Beorhtnoth's death. According to the *Liber Eliensis*, among the rich gifts bestowed by his widow, Ælfflæd, was an embroidery (now lost) depicting his great deeds.

head had been hacked off

Other grisly discoveries were reported in James Bentham's letter to the Society of Antiquaries in 1772:

> It is a curious fact (given to the Editor by a Gentleman present when the bones were examined), that the *clavicula*, or collar bone, found in Brithnoth's Cell, appeared to have been nearly cut through – with, perhaps, a battle axe, or a two-handed sword (Deegan 291).

very many had fallen on both sides

A precise body count is of course impossible to ascertain. E.V. Gordon thought the poem to be 'generally trustworthy' on the facts of the battle, while other sources could be prone to hyperbole, especially on the matter of the depletion of the viking forces. The *Vita Oswaldi*'s claim that 'the Danes... scarcely had men enough left to man the ships' is, according to Gordon, 'certainly an exaggeration', for they were able to 'continue plundering along the coasts' soon after (5–7).

Torhthelm (colloquially Totta).... Tídwald (in short Tída)

I have not found in Tolkien's papers any indication of the provenance or special significance of the names of the two chief voices in *The Homecoming*. While Totta was early settled upon, replacing Pudda in the earliest drafts, Tída emerges later, and in stages: Tibba > Tudda > Tída from Version *H* on. Tom Shippey glosses Torhthelm, 'bright helmet' and Tídwald, 'ruler of time' ('Tolkien and the Homecoming' 326). Jessica

Yates has made the fascinating observation that the names have been 'staring us in the face' in the Old English poem *Crist* – '*Torht ofer tunglas, þu Tida gehwane*' – only three lines down from the famous '*Eala earendel*', which can be said to have launched Tolkien's mythology. Balancing one another on opposite sides of the caesura, they may capture a kind of *Homecoming* dialogue in miniature. Other theories might draw on English place-names. Tidwalditun certainly makes an impression as the former name of Heybridge, not far from Maldon in Essex. The villages of Little and Great Totham lie only a few miles north of Heybridge. Farther afield is Totanæs (now Totnes) in Devon, or Tottenham of north London.

heroes of northern antiquity
Such figures, straddling history and legend, were often at the heart of Tolkien's own studies. There is a wistful pleasure in eavesdropping on Tída and Totta, in an age when, perhaps, such tales were better preserved. For more on such legends, see also *Finn and Hengest*, and Tolkien's discussion of Fróda in 'On Fairy-stories' (*MC* 127).

Ælfwine
The name, meaning 'Elf-friend', plays a major role in Tolkien's legendarium, most plainly as the Anglo-Saxon mariner of *The Book of Lost Tales*. If Ælfwine's part recedes in later revisions of the mythology, the concept of the Elf-friend certainly does not. Elf-friends, from Elendil to Bilbo, function within the frame as protagonists in the adventures and without it as the authors and transmitters of the tales themselves.

It is here implied...
This point is elaborated in '*Beowulf*: The Monsters and the

Critics'. Tolkien notes that Beorhtwold's 'doctrinal expression' of northern courage 'may well have been actually used by the *eald geneat*, but none the less (or perhaps rather precisely on that account) is probably to be regarded not as new-minted, but as an ancient and honoured *gnome* of long descent' (*MC* 45 n11).

rhyme: presaging the fading end of the old heroic alliterative measure…

For more on Cnut's verse and its connections to Ely Abbey, see Eleanor Parker's 'Merry sang the monks'. For further discussion of rhyme in *Maldon*, see Appendix II, section (e).

little if at all freer

Tolkien hypothesizes at some length about different OE verse modes in 'The Tradition of Versification'. On a half sheet between pages 7 and 8 of this essay, he classifies three types: 1) '*Strict epic or 'fornyrðislag' type*'; 2) '*Freer verse*'; and 3) '*Poetic or emotional prose*'. *Maldon* he called the 'chief example' of the freer type 2, whose hallmarks included 'greater freedom in 2nd half anacrusis not infrequent, head-stave occasionally on 2nd beat in 2nd half – especially when assisted by crossed alliteration which was considerably used. Heavy types and loose types commoner' (fol. 39).

Historia Eliensis

The *Liber Eliensis* is a twelfth-century history of Ely Abbey in Latin, beginning with its founding in 673.

King Canute

Neither the sporting resistance of Beorhtnoth nor the monetary tribute of Æthelred II would long hold off the Northern invaders. The fierce but Christian Canute (or Cnut) became

King of England in 1016, and later claimed the crowns of
Denmark and Sweden, ruling a vast – but short lived – North
Sea Empire, which collapsed with his death in 1035.

(II)
THE HOMECOMING OF BEORHTNOTH
BEORHTHELM'S SON

The sound is heard...in the darkness.
In 'On Fairy-stories', Tolkien remarks that fantasy 'hardly ever
succeeds in Drama...visibly and audibly acted' (140). Perhaps
this is why little to nothing is seen in Tolkien's verse drama.
But like Tída's dark lantern, *The Homecoming* can illuminate
the fabric of Tolkien's fantasy.

barrow-wights
These spirits haunting ancient burial mounds feature in the
opening verses collected in *The Adventures of Tom Bombadil* and
in the early misadventures of the hobbits in 'Fog on the Barrow
Downs', the eighth chapter of *The Fellowship of the Ring*.

gleeman's stuff
A gleeman is a professional singer, perhaps a descendent of
the OE *scop* or bard. Tída refers to Totta's family business with
a note of disparagement.

Woden's days
That is, in pre-Christian England. Woden is Old English for
the Norse god, Odin.

they'll be two-leggéd
Wolf and outlaw intertwine in Old Norse (*vargr*) and Old
English (*wearh*), and this connection is revived also in the

evil wargs of *The Lord of the Rings*. In meeting the scavengers shortly thereafter, Tída's suggestion here proves true. See also note on *Maldon* l. 91 in Part Two.

Owls are omens
This difference of opinion on the bird offers an opportune moment to note that *The Homecoming* shares some common ground with medieval debate poems such as the Middle English *Owl and the Nightingale*, which Tolkien studied, translated, and taught at various times during his career.

His sister-son!
For more on this special relationship, see Tolkien's note on *Maldon* l. 115 in Part Two below.

gather them ungrown
This poignant image recalls *A Spring Harvest*, a collection of G.B. Smith's poetry edited by Tolkien, and published in 1918, following Smith's untimely death in the First World War. Mark Atherton has noted parallels between Smith's 'Glastonbury' and *The Homecoming* (*There and Back Again* 158).

bad when bearded men put shield at back....the dastards
A reference to the flight of Odda's sons recounted in the poem. See Tolkien's note in Part Two on *Maldon* l. 190.

new weapon of the old metal
Ælfwine here is described in terms of a sword reforged – a familiar trope in Tolkien's legendarium, as in Narsil > Andúril and Anglachel > Gurthang.

left with the luggage
In *The Lord of the Rings*, the hobbits make self-deprecating

comments in such terms. Sam on the Great River deems him-self 'no more than luggage in a boat'; and Pippin, captured by the Uruk-hai, takes a gloomy look at his role in the company: 'a nuisance: a passenger, a piece of luggage' (383, 445).

a poor freeman may prove...more tough...than titled earls
Doubts about Totta's courage notwithstanding, the sentiment, full of loyalty and unexpected pluck, is surely hobbit-like. In a 1955 letter to W.H. Auden, Tolkien notes 'the value of Hobbits, in putting earth under the feet of "romance", and in provid-ing subjects for "ennoblement" and heroes more praiseworthy than the professionals' (*Letters* 215).

count back their kin to kings ere Woden
Some of the more fanciful family trees of the Anglo-Saxon Chronicle do just that.

the bite of swords
Tolkien's *Beowulf* translation likewise reads that the hero's sword 'would bite not' Grendel's mother (1.1273). It is a familiar image in Tolkien's legends, notably in the sentient Gurthang's appetite for blood in the Tale of Túrin Turambar and the blade of Gondolin, simply called, by the Goblins in *The Hobbit*, Biter.

eyes...as Grendel's in the moon
Gordon argues that '*Maldon* is of the same school as *Beowulf* and nearer to *Beowulf* in heroic art and social feeling than any other Old English poem' (23). Here Tolkien suggests that while Totta does not know battle, he does know some *Beowulf*. In draft version *C*, 'Grendel's' replaces in pencil the more generic 'a fen-dweller's' (*MS. Tolkien 5* fol. 10).

his sword....the golden hilts.
For the development of this scene in the drafts, see Appendix V. See also the introduction to Mark Atherton's *Battle of Maldon*. In the fairy-tale *Sellic Spell*, the hero Beewolf comes to be called 'the knight of the golden hilts' (403).

Now mourn forever....while word or woe in the world lasteth.
The dirge, as Tída notes, owes much to the end of *Beowulf*.

You laboured long...in the watches of the night
In 'The Tradition of Versification', Tolkien writes of the *Maldon* poet's likely participation in such a lonely vigil. It was also part of his own routine. In a 1944 letter to Christopher Tolkien on the progress of *The Lord of the Rings*, he notes: 'I have seriously embarked on an effort to finish my book, and have been sitting up rather late' (70). The phrase, 'watches of the night', occurs more than once in the Rohan chapters of *The Lord of the Rings*.

If swords he was seeking, he soon found one, by the biting end.
This plainly echoes (or anticipates) the exchange between Beorhtnoth and the messenger in the OE poem (see also Part Two, note on *Maldon* l. 46).

sprinkled
Baptized – converted to Christianity.

By Edmund's head
Edmund the Martyr, East Anglian king, was beheaded by vikings more than a century before the Battle of Maldon.

his funeral ale
Ceremonial beer drunk at the funeral feast. Tolkien memorably describes *Beowulf* in such terms in 'On Translating *Beowulf*'. Defending the poem from 'one famous critic' who claimed that the poem was only 'small beer', he counters: 'Yet if beer at all, it is a drink dark and bitter: a solemn funeral -ale with the taste of death' (*MC* 49).

It's strange to me how they came across this causeway
For the developments of this crucial scene, see Appendix V.

to give minstrels matter for mighty songs
Beorhtnoth does, after a fashion, succeed in this.

So the last is fallen... In olden days this isle conquered
Totta's verse plainly echoes the closing lines of *The Battle of Brunanburh*, a Chronicle poem commemorating a victory in 937. But here, rather than celebrating the continuity with the glorious conquest of the fifth century, Beorhtnoth's fall seems to represent the end of an era. One of the modern touches of *The Homecoming* is its recognition of the cyclical irony to the depredations of the Danes in this time; centuries before, under leaders like Hengest and Horsa, it was the 'English Vikings' who played the role of invader. One sobering constant in all these centuries of war would seem to be, as Tída notes, that the poor 'must die and dung' the land.

perish all pirates
See Part Two, note on translating *wicinga* (*Maldon* l. 26).

No dirge for them
The *Maldon* poet's work does manage to record the words and brave deeds of more than just noble retainers. If we follow the

conceit of Totta's eventual authorship of the poem, we might see him learning from Tída here and elsewhere, as in the case of acknowledging the tactical blunder at the causeway.

But Æthelred'll prove less easy prey...
Totta's hopeful prediction, of course, does not come off.

faithful servant
A collocation used of Sam and Gollum in *The Lord of the Rings*.

It's dark!....doom shall come and dark conquer.
Anna Smol sees Totta's dream vision 'penetrating to the heart of heroic tradition' ('Bodies in War' 275). The striking imagery certainly recalls that of Tolkien's famous *Beowulf* lecture:

> as in a little circle of light about their halls, men with courage as their stay went forward to that battle with the hostile world and the offspring of the dark which ends for all, even the kings and champions, in defeat (*MC* 18).

For more on the development of this dream sequence, see Appendix V.

my dream shattered
The whole night's experience has been a kind of bump in the road for Totta.

your words were queer....I don't hold with that.
Tída here coolly dismisses the most famous lines in OE verse.

Dirige, Domine...
The chant is part of the Catholic Office of the Dead, entreating God to direct the way home. While it may not be the

homecoming that Beorhtnoth had in mind, nor is it that of the hopeless Northern heroism.

A Voice in the dark

Perhaps the clearest stage direction for the voice comes in the draft held at Leeds. As the Dirige chant dies down, 'a louder voice (on a boat with several men in it comes in gloom past front of stage) is heard saying the English words'.

In 'The Tradition of Versification', Tolkien doubts that rhymes like that of *Maldon* l. 271 came from the poet; it seems 'detachable', as if 'it has slipped in from a different style'. He may have been thinking along the same lines in preparing for the BBC production of his play, thinking it 'best to omit' the voice in the dark, though in the end an actor is hired to play the part (*Chronology* 467–9). The mysterious voice from the water is nonetheless a fixture from the early drafts of *The Homecoming*, gaining additional jarring potency as the rest of the drama moves from rhyme to alliteration.

Tolkien's attribution of the source – the lines 'echo...some verses...referring to King Canute' – only gets us so far. The festive occasion is reversed in *The Homecoming* – the monks sing not merrily but 'sadly'. And Canute's rise to power is still a long way off at the time of Tída and Totta's quest; he may not have even been born when Maldon was fought. Whatever their ultimate portent, the jingle of rhyme pulls us from the alliterative tradition and, in the call to listen a while, our attention returns to the business of interpretation, the effort to 'hear the tears through the harps twanging'. For further discussion of the historical resonances here, see West's 'Canute and Beorhtnoth' (350–353).

(III)
OFERMOD

But to merit a place in *Essays and Studies*...
The verse drama appears to long pre-date the essay, though
how hastily it might have been composed is unclear; at any
rate no extant draft material for 'Ofermod' is held with the
rest of the manuscripts in the Bodleian Library.

'the only purely heroic poem extant in Old English'
The quotation is derived from E.V. Gordon's 1937 edition (24).

eschewing weapons
'I have learned, too, that this fierce slayer in his savagery to
weapons gives no heed. I too then will disdain (so love me
Hygelac, my liege lord!) to bear either sword, or wide shield'
(*Beowulf* l. 349–352).

**as wisdom might direct even a hero to do... a long
'vaunt'**
This emphasis on strategy and the ethical obligations of a
leader in combat is, as Tolkien notes, only one of many ingredients to be considered. Tolkien's 1938 New Year's Day talk on
'Dragons' views the hero's decision in another light:

> 'Beowulf seems to have realized the nature of dragons: that
> their power grows to match power, so that they can destroy
> hosts and are usually only to be defeated by lonely courage.
> He was a king, but he refused to take an army'. ('Dragons' 52).

The vaunt in question sees a 'fearless' Beowulf describe the
unfortunate necessity of arms and instruct his men not to
engage in this deed beyond their 'measure', but to wait on the
hill (*Beowulf* l. 2109–2129).

treat a desperate battle…as a sporting match
For more on this temptation, see Appendix VI.

tales and verse of poets now lost save for echoes
Tolkien's taste for lost tales remains a constant in his scholarly and creative work.

Too foolish to be heroic
There is in all this discussion of the perils of courageous excess a connection to Tolkien's own surname, which could mean 'foolhardy' or, as Tolkien adapted it for a character in *The Notion Club Papers*, 'Rashbold'. In a letter to Houghton Mifflin Tolkien wrote:

> My name is TOLKIEN (*not -kein*). It is a German name (from Saxony), an anglicization of *Tollkiehn*, i.e. *tollkühn*. But, except as a guide to spelling, this fact is as fallacious as all facts in the raw. For I am neither 'foolhardy' nor German, whatever some remote ancestors may have been.

For more on the recurrence of this attribute in Tolkien's career and the name in various guises in his fiction, see Fisher.

if the poem had any rounded ending
Tolkien speculates on a length up to 600 lines (see Part Three).

The Charge of the Light Brigade
Alfred, Lord Tennyson poem written shortly after the disastrous charge in the 1854 Battle of Balaclava.

even in spite of themselves
If Totta goes on to compose the OE poem, we can well imagine the severe criticism of Beorhtnoth made 'in spite of' himself.

the *snotere ceorlas*

Tolkien's gloss is 'wise men'. They find 'little fault' in Beowulf's decision to aid Hrothgar – 'i.e. they applauded it' (l.163–64, p. 110).

Wita scal gepyldig...

Lines 65–69 of the OE poem, *The Wanderer*. Tolkien rendered them thus in an unpublished translation:

> A sage (a counsellor) must be long suffering, not too fiery of heart must he be, not too hasty in speech, not too soft in war, not too thoughtless in heart, not too fearful and afraid, not too greedy of wealth, not too eager to boast ere he have clear knowledge (*MS. Tolkien A 38/1*, fol. 14).

PART TWO

The Battle of Maldon

INTRODUCTORY NOTE

[The following note draws from Tolkien's wide-ranging introductory comments on the poem (Bodleian Library *MS. Tolkien A 30/2* fols. 74–83). It has been edited to provide, in Tolkien's own words, a brief indication of *Maldon*'s textual history and literary interest. The material here dates to the mid-to-late 1920s, when Tolkien delivered lectures first on 'The Verse of Sweet's *Anglo-Saxon Reader*' (Michaelmas 1926) and later on *Maldon* (1928 and 1930).]

Manuscript (Cotton Otho A XII) was almost entirely destroyed by fire on Oct. 23, 1731. The manuscript was really a composite bundle of manuscripts of quite different nature and periods. Its contents can be seen described in Wanley's *Catalogue*.... He adds excerpts from the *Historia Eliensis* concerning the life of Byrhtnoth.

And that is all we should know about the poem, but for a fortunate chance: Thomas Hearne an eminent eighteenth-century antiquarian printed it in 1726 (in a hotch-potch appendix containing strangely assorted matter often of little bearing on the matter of the book):

Johannis Confratris & Monachi Glastoniensis Chronica.
I have a copy here if anyone wishes to see it.

Throughout Old English literature this is the case
– almost every survival is of radical importance. *Deor's
Lament* – Strophe! *Waldere* – wide cycle of Gmc. legends
vigorously heated! Lyrics, Riddles. *Maldon.* Revises 2
opinions 1) Practice of alliterative verse was not W.S. 2)
that it was already hopelessly decrepit in tenth century.

This piece has been thought to be the work of a poet
knocking off vigorous verse in the heat of the events – and
incidentally writing two lines memorable as the best and
most concise statement of the heroic Northern spirit.

We have no knowledge who wrote this poem – it has
come down to us in the ordinary form of Old English verse:
West Saxon with occasional non-West Saxon forms – here
also with decisive signs of lateness...and also complicated
by the errors of an eighteenth century antiquarian whose
knowledge of Old English was very small. It may have been
an Essex man, or even a man of Byrhtnoth's house. Beorhtnoth or in late form Byrhtnoth was Ealdorman of Essex.

The language of old lays is used but it is to be remembered that life still in many ways was true to this language.
Beorhtnoth was a man of great rank, with his own retinue and following bound by personal ties to himself and
his house, as well as an emphatic 'duke', a king's chief-
officer, whose fame and valour won him respect all over
the kingdom. Such deaths as Byrhtnoth's are of more
import than all the victories of imperial armies since
the world began. From them real literature springs – the
literature quickened by true human sentiment (so like and
so utterly different from its counterfeits).

Taken out of the hurried but moving and impassioned words of this chance fragment his last speech even in this age (shy even when believing of sayings above a whisper) rings movingly true. He died in defence of his lord, England, and Christendom thanking God for all joys of life. And this thing preserved (by chance?!) survives to overthrow the text-book estimate of the England of Æthelred and lets in more light than any other document upon the grievous struggles and disasters and the heroism of the English. It took some 300 years of misery to quench them. What Byrhtnoth did unsung – What songs of Byrhtnoth have been lost! What a waste of broad lands, good things of England, proud lives – and the gain a few moving lines that can still stir the roots of the hearts of people who will take the trouble to learn the language. The heart may be moved by many other things – but there is perhaps no thrill so salutary as that which comes from catching with sympathetic ear lectures of the voices of one's own people from far down the years in what was England and is (perhaps) England still.

Maldon is not only a thing which has some intrinsic interest of its own, it has now an accidental interest in recalling the feelings and the code of conduct and the desperate struggles of men in England very long ago. It offers a disturbing glimpse sufficient to prove that we know very little of the history and fate of the native [?forms of] verse in England before 1100.

THE BATTLE OF MALDON, PROSE TRANSLATION BY J.R.R. TOLKIEN

[Belonging to the same period is a complete manuscript draft of a translation of *Maldon* (Bodleian Library *MS. Tolkien A 30/2*, fols. 124–36) in ink. A pencilled note, badly smudged at the top left of the translation's first page reads: 'this ... affair ...intended ... attempt to reproduce the poetic effect of the original'. It is my guess that the missing words would rather reverse the significance of the note, for the text plainly is *not* concerned with poetic effect but with the struggle to pin down with some precision the poet's narrative. What is left is the rousing tale, here in Tolkien's own words, that inspired *The Homecoming*.

In editing the manuscript, I have chosen to present it as clearly and continuously as possible, adopting many emendations silently, and presenting Tolkien's occasional queries or explanatory asides as footnotes. The manuscript numbers in the left margin every 5 lines of the poem are in blue pencil; I give these line markers in brackets to help orient readers who refer to the OE text.]

TRANSLATION
BATTLE OF MALDON

[1]... would be broken. He then commanded each man to abandon his horse and drive it off, and to march forward, giving his mind to handstrokes* and to good courage. As [5] soon as the kinsman of Offa perceived that the earl would not brook cowardice, he let then his beloved hawk fly from his hand away to the wood, and he strode to battle; by which token it was plain to see that the young man would not show faint heart [10] in that struggle, since he (now) took to arms. And Eadric too purposed to aid his chief and lord in battle; he marched forward keen with spear to war: a loyal heart had he as long as he might hold in hands shield or broad sword; [15] he made good his vow, now that he must fight in the front rank before his lord.

There then Byrhtnoth began to dispose his men and rode from point to point giving advice and orders, how they should place themselves and hold [20] that position, and bade men hold their shields up rightly and have no fear. When he had well ordered that host he dismounted amongst his men, where he loved best to be, where the men of his own household were, of whose loyalty he was most certain.

[25] Then there stood upon the banks and fiercely cried, speaking these words, the messenger of pirates, who boastfully announced to the chief the business of the enemy from overseas, where he stood upon that shore:

---

* (i.e. hand to hand fighting with the enemy)

'Bold seafarers have sent me to you, and have bidden [30] me say to you: that quickly must you send rings (of gold) if you would save yourselves;* and it is better for you (all) that you should buy off this onslaught with tribute than we should meet in so deadly a battle. We need not destroy one another, if you have means for this [35] we will in exchange for the gold make a binding truce. If you,† who are the chief man here, decide upon this, that you will save your people, and give to the seamen money at their own assessment in return for friendship and accept terms of peace from us,‡ we will [40] then go aboard with that pay-ment and put out to sea (again) and keep peace with you'.

Byrhtnoth spake, and upraised his shield, and shook his pliant spear-shaft, and uttered these words, wroth, undaunted, he gave him answer. [45] 'Do you hear, pirate, what this people says? They will for tribute give you spears, the venomed point, swords forged of old – such war gear as will be of little good to you in battle. Envoy of our ene-mies from oversea, go back and declare this to them, [50] tell your people§ a tale much less pleasant, that here stands no craven lord among his company, one who will defend this his native land, the realm of Æthelred my master; this people and this earth; the heathen shall [55] fall in battle. A mean welcome it seems to me that you should go back onboard with our money unfought; now that you have come here from so far away and set foot inside our

---

* (let rings set against, in exchange, for protection)
† (whoever you are)
‡ = make peace with us
§ or princes

land; not so easily shall you win treasure – spearpoint and sword blade, and the grim game of war shall [60] first decide our quarrel before we give tribute!'

He then gave orders to advance the ranks, and for the men to march forwards so that they all stood upon the river bank. There because of the water neither host could get at the other; [65] there after the ebb came the flowing tide, the streaming waters locked together.* They were impatient for the time when they might meet spear with spear. They (then) stood there on either side of the River Panta in their armies, the ranks of Essex and the pirate horde, and neither [70] side could damage the other, save for such as got his death by flying arrow. The tide went out. The seamen stood ready, many pirates eager for battle. Then the protector of warriors† ordered a [75] soldier bold in battle (Wulfstan was his name; he was Ceola's son and a valiant man among his own people) to hold the bridge, and he shot with his casting-spear the first man who there, more daring than the others, set foot upon the bridge. There stood there beside Wulfstan two soldiers [80] proud and fearless, Ælfhere and Maccus: It was not in their mind to beat a retreat at that ford, nay, stoutly they defended themselves against the enemy as long as they could wield weapons.

When then they‡ perceived this and saw clearly that they had there [85] come upon no gentle guardians of the bridge, those vile invaders made a plausible appeal (to

---

* (joined – of the river & the incoming tide)

† commander

‡ (the Danes)

Byrhtnoth's chivalry) and asked they might have oppor-
tunity for coming up on his bank and leading their troops
over the ford. Then the earl* in his overconfident chivalry
[90] conceded too much land to that hateful people. Then
did he, Byrhthelm's son, shout over the fatal water (and
men hearkened to him): 'Now we have made room for
you, come ye men, quickly to us and to battle. God alone
[95] knoweth who may be masters of the stricken field'.

Then waded those murderous wolves,† (all) the pirate
host, heedless of the water, west over the Panta, and over
the clear water the men of the invading fleet bore their
[100] linden shields. There to meet his foes stood ready
Byrhtnoth with his men, he ordered them to make that
phalanx‡ with their shields and bade his host stand firm
against the enemy. Now was fighting near at hand, glory
in battle; the time was come when those whose fate it was
[105] to die should there fall slain. There was the battle cry
upraised, the ravens went to and fro, and the eagle eager
for carrion; clamour was upon the earth. Then they let fly
from their hands spears file-hardened and javelins ground§
sharp. [110] Bows were busy, shield received point, bitter
was that onslaught; men fell on either side, and warriors
lay dead. Wounded was Wulfmær, Byrhtnoth's kinsman his
sister's son, and he laid him on his deathbed amid the
slain, [115] grievously hewn was he with swords. There was
a payment for him returned to the pirates. It is said that

---

* (Byrhtnoth)
† (outcasts outlaws)
‡ (British square)
§ (grimly)

Eadweard slew one of them quickly with his sword (nor did he hesitate in his stroke) so that dead at his feet the doomed warrior fell. [120] For this his prince* spoke his thanks to him, to his own retainer, when he had space. Thus the stouthearted men stood firm in battle, and bethought them eagerly who might first with (spear) point reach the vitals [125] of men doomed to die, and fight with their weapons.† The dead fell upon the earth.

Steadfast they stood, Byrhtnoth steadied them, bidding each man give his mind to valorous deeds who desired to win him glory in battle with the Danes. Then advanced [130] one hardy in battle, and lifted up his weapon and his shield before him, and strode against the warrior (Byrhtnoth). Equally resolute did the earl advance to meet the churl,‡ each purposed ill to the other. Then let fly the seaman [135] a southern spear, so that the lord of warriors (Byrhtnoth) was wounded; he gave a quick thrust with his shield so that the spear shaft burst asunder, and he caused the spearhead to fly off so that it sprang back. Enraged was the (English) warrior, he stabbed the proud pirate with his spear who had given him that wound. War-wise was the warrior of the (English) host. He let [140] his dart pass through the man's neck, his hand guided it so that it reached the vitals of that fierce ravager.§ Then speedily he cast at another so that his corslet was broken, and he was wounded in [145] his breast through the linked rings,

---

* (Byrhtnoth)

† (i.e. they thought only of using their weapons to best advantage and doing hurt to foes)

‡ >man

§ (lit. reach the life in)

at his heart stood the venomed point. The gladder was the chief; then laughed aloud that high hearted man, and cried thanks to God for that day's work that the Lord had granted to him. Then one of the Danish men let fly a javelin from his hands and gripe and [150] it reached and pierced the thane of Æthelred. At his side there stood a youth not yet grown to manhood, a boy in battle, and he boldly snatched the bloodstained spear [155] from Byrhtnoth – he was Wulfmær the young son of Wulfstan; he let it grimly hard fly back again. In passed the point so that he now lay dead on the earth who had so grievously smitten his lord.

Then a man in armour approached the wounded lord, he thought [160] to get the warrior's rings and raiment and his amulets and his jewelled sword. Then Byrhtnoth swept out his sword from his sheath – broad and burnished was its blade and smote him upon his coat of mail. All too quickly did that* pirate warrior hinder his stroke, and maimed [165] the chieftain's arm. Then fell to the earth the sword with pale gleaming hilt; he could not hold his strong sword nor wield his weapon. Still he spoke this speech more, the grey haired warrior, and enheartened his men, bidding them advance [170] together like brave men. Then he could no longer stand firm upon his feet, and he cast his eyes up to Heaven (and said) 'I thank Thee, Lord of peoples, for all those joys that I have known [175] in this world. Now I have, O merciful God, the greatest need that Thou vouchsafe the grace unto my spirit that my soul may journey to Thee, into thy dominion, King of Angels,

---

* (? or some other)

passing in peace. I entreat Thee [180] that adversaries of Hell oppress me not'. Then the heathen men smote him and both those that stood by him, Ælfnoth and Wulfmær, both lay dead, together with their lord they gave up their lives.

[185] Then those left the field who had no heart to remain; there Odda's sons were the first to take to flight from the battle, and Godric abandoned that good patron who had oft given him many a horse. He leapt upon that [190] steed that was his master's own, in those very trappings of his, in which it was not right (that he should appear),* and his two brothers both galloped off with him, Godwine and Godwig, they cared no more for the battle but went from the fighting and made for the wood flying into fast places, and saving their lives, and (with them) more men than would [195] ever have been thought fit had they remembered all those things deserving their gratitude he had done to their good – even as Offa had one day ere that battle declared in the place of council, when Byrhtnoth held an assembly (of his [200] captains) that many there spoke manly who later in need would not stand firm.

Now was slain the chieftain of the host, Æthelred's captain; all the men of his house saw [205] that their lord lay low. Still the proud thanes advanced, fearless men with eager hearts, they hastened on – all desired but one of two things: to lay down their lives or avenge him they loved. To this did Ælfwine the son of Ælfric exhort them, a knight young in years, these were the words he spoke, [210] and valiantly he said: 'Remember all those speeches that we

---

* because it caused panic

have often spoken at the drinking of mead, when we warriors sitting in the hall have made brave vows concerning
[215] hard fields to be fought: Now may it be put to the
test who is bold. I will here prove to all my good blood
that am come of a great house in Mercia, mine grandsire
Ealhelm was named, a wise ealdorman (duke), blessed
among men. Nor shall the nobles in [220] that people
reproach me saying that I willing left this host to go back
to mine own home, now that my chief lies stricken to
death in battle; greatest of all griefs is that to me. He was
both my kinsman and lord of my allegiance. [225] Then
he advanced (against the enemy) forgetting not his desire
for vengeance, until with his spear point he got there upon
one of those seamen in their host, so that he lay upon the
ground overcome by his weapon. Then did he exhort his
own men, friends and comrades, that they [230] should
advance.

Offa spoke, shaking his spear of ashwood: 'Lo thou,
Ælfwine, hast admonished us all as there was need; now
that our chief lies slain upon the earth, it behooves us
all to encourage each the other to brave fighting [235] so
long as a man may hold and grasp a weapon, hard brand,
spear and good sword. Godric, craven son of Odda, has
betrayed us all; [240] when he rode off on that horse, on
that steed proudly caparisoned, all too many men thought
that it was our master, wherefore on this field have ranks
been opened, and the shield wall broken. Curse on his
leaving* that he should set in flight so many of our men!'

---

* (let perish his initiative! – more probably a curse than say 'may it
fail!' since it has succeeded)

Leofsunu spake and upraised his buckler, his shield as his [245] guard, and thus he spake in answer to the other. 'This do I vow: that I will not flee hence a foot's pace, but will advance and avenge in battle my patron and my lord. No cause shall have trusty men about Sturmere to reproach me [250] saying that when my leader fell I went home masterless and left the fight; nay! arms shall be my death – point and iron.' In wrath he strode forth, unyielding he fought on, and did not deign to flee. Dunnere, [255] a simple "ceorl", then brandished a javelin, called aloud for all to hear, crying that every man should avenge Byrhtnoth: 'no man may show faint heart who thinks to avenge his lord amid the host, nor may he reck for his life'.

Then they went forth, they cared not for [260] their lives; fiercely did the men of his household put them into the fight, those grim wielders of the spears, and God they prayed that they might avenge their lord and patron, and compass a slaughter among their foes. [265] Gallantly did the hostage come to their aid – Ecglaf's son, Æschferð* by name; he showed no faint heart in that play of war, but many an arrow he sent flying forth; now he hit a shield, now he wounded his man, unceasingly [270] from time to time he wounded one of them so long as he could wield weapons.

Moreover still in the forefront stood Eadweard the Tall† ready, eager; vaunting words he spake that he would [275] not flee nor give back a foot's measure of land now a better man than he lay dead. He broke their shield

---

* (not Unferð)
† (Long Edward cf. Edward I = longshanks)

wall and fought with them until he had nobly avenged his patron upon those seamen, ere he too lay among the slain. So too did Æthelric, [280] a noble of Byrhtnoth's retinue, a gallant man who hung never back, unwearyingly he fought, Sibyrht's brother,* and many another too they clove the hollow shields, boldly they defended themselves; shieldrim was burst; corslet sang a [285] grim song. Then in battle slew Offa that† sea-pirate, and he fell upon the earth, and there the kinsman of Gadd laid him down. Swiftly in that fight was then Offa hewn down; yet he had accomplished that which he promised to his lord, even as he had vowed before with regard to his [290] patron, that they would both ride back to town safe to their homes or (together) fall in the host, and perish of their wounds upon the stricken field; he lay like a good knight close to his prince.

Then was there a splintering of shields, the men [295] from the sea strode on filled with the rage of war; oft did the spear invade the house of life of doomed man.‡ Then Wi(h)stan stepped forth, Thurstan's son, and fought against them; he was the death of three of them in that press ere he laid him down among [300] the slain, the son of Wighelm he was. It was a grim encounter there that day: fighting the men stood fast in that struggle; warriors fell dead, heavy with wounds; the dead fell upon the earth. All that while Oswold and Ealdwold, those [305]

---

* probably = Æthelric

† (which? That one who killed Byrhtnoth?)

‡ (i.e. again and again did their spears pierce the bodies of the English remnant and wound them mortally)

THE BATTLE OF MALDON

two brothers, held the men together, and bade their kins-
men there in the hour of need to stand, unyielding to ply
their weapons.

Byrhtwold spake, his shield he raised, an old retainer
was he* [310] his ash-spear he shook, and right boldly he
admonished them thus: 'Each mind shall be the sterner,
heart the bolder, each our spirit greater as our strength
lessens! Here lies our good chief all hewn to [315] death
upon the sand; forever may he weep who now thinks to
leave this fight, I am old and have seen much of life; I
will not go from here, but I think to lie at the side of my
master, whom I loved so well!' Thus too did Godric [320]
Æthelgar's son exhort them all to fight: again and again
he sent a spear and deadly shaft flying against the pirates,
as he strode in the foremost ranks of the host, hewing and
hurting until he too fell in battle – that was not that [325]
Godric that forsook the field...

---

* (he had grown old in the service of arms in noble household)

NOTES

[In addition to the material above, Tolkien also penned a substantial set of notes on the poem, organized by line number (Bodleian *Tolkien MS 30/2*, fols. 84–123). The limited selection presented here highlights the range of Tolkien's interests in the history, language, and narrative of the poem, though much technical linguistic detail is omitted. To better orient the reader, and in keeping with Christopher Tolkien's practice in *Beowulf: A Translation and Commentary*, the line number and OE text in question follow the corresponding phrase from Tolkien's translation.]

the earl [would not brook cowardice]; 6 *se eorl*
Apparently only used of *Byrhtnoð* in this poem. Originally *eorl* meant one of good or noble blood, but not necessarily of any high rank or distinction. In the older heroic (aristocratic) verse it is practically synonymous with full grown fighting man. The same word became in Scandinavia much enhanced, and meant powerful local chief or man of rank next to king. Here we see probable influence of this Scand[inavian] use (*earl*, later *jarl*) on *eorl*, which has produced modern *earl*.

[the messenger of] pirates; 26 *wicinga*
Only in *Maldon* in verse. Occurs ll. 26, 73, 97, 116, 139, 322.

This popularity reflects contemporary conditions. The word meant exactly what we mean by *pirate*: a *víkingr* in Scand [inavian]. Was quite ready to attack people in his own home if *rich.* In one saga (*Hallfreðar*) we have their version of the high-wayman's 'your money or your life'. They said 'your money *and* your life'. *Sokki* the *víkingr* set fire to Þorvald's house (because Þorvaldr was well off). What injury have I done to you' said Þ. 'We vikings don't worry about that sort of thing – we want your life and your money'. He got it.

Honourable profession – especially for younger sons, or such as had got into scrapes at home. Its original sense is contested – at this time = pirate and is so glossed. One viking witnessing an English charter signs himself *arch-pirata*, pirate-chief.

at their own assessment; 38 *on hyra sylfra dom*
An old Germanic expression...

It naturally connoted complete control of the one that had 'self-doom' and a pretty handsome payment. To give anyone 'self-doom' was either an act of generosity = help yourself – or an acknowledgement of wrong, or defeat.

In a free community (such as Iceland) it often arrived at justice since a generous offer of 'self-doom' forced by public opinion the acceptor to be generous in assessment. In this kind of context it implies however tyrannical greed.

Byrhtnoth spake, and upraised his shield; 42 *Byrhtnoð maþelode, bord hafenode*
An early type of rhyming phrase. This sort *with alliteration* and rhyme thrown in as an occasional adornment is to be found in the older poetry. It is distinct, but paves way for rhyme without alliteration cf. 271, 282.

wroth, undaunted; 44 *yrre and anræd*
Evidently traditional – cf. *Beowulf* 1575; *an-ræd* may also have existed = fierce to go on, cf. *an-mod* = unanimous.

They will for tribute give you spears; 46 *Hi willað eow to gafole garas syllan*
The 'treasure' of tribute often took form of rings, mail, and war-equipment. The joke here is that B[yrhtnoth] says 'they will give them as tribute spears, bitter spears, and ancient swords and that sort of war-gear that is (or will be) no use to you in battle'. A double-barrelled joke. The giving will take form of smiting them; the war-gear will be on wrong side.

the venomed point; 47 *ættrynne ord*
Meant especially spear-point but it was sometimes used of swords. Here it means stabbing weapons in general.

[swords forged of] old; 47 *ealde*
A compliment. Archaeology seems to confirm that the Germanic fashion of swords declined in England, and that it was fact, as well as legendary attribution to *Wēland*, etc., that made a good sword be called *eald*.

Battles are won by old swords. Beowulf and the *eald sweord eotenisc* [In Tolkien's translation: 'a blade gigantic, old, with edges stern...the work of giants'.] with which B[eowulf] finished off the Grendel-family, 1558. Offa (Uffo) won his battle with *Skrep* [sword used by Offa, a figure of legend alluded to in *Beowulf* and *Widsith*].

[such] war gear; 48 *heregeatu*
Became the technical term for 'equipment' esp. 'apparel' granted by lord to a vassal, and going back to lord on vassal's death – extended to include horses cf. 188 where B[yrhtnoth] is referred to as *hlaford* of Godric – and becomes in end a tribute payable to lord of a manor on the decease of a tenant.

spearpoint and sword blade; 60 ***ord and ecg***
Synecdoche: *ord,* point = spear; *ecg,* edge = sword

The grim jest is that '*ord and ecg*' shall be our judges and arbitrators, and shall decide our quarrel before we come to the point of paying.

streaming waters locked together; 66 *lucon lagustreamas*
The streams of the sea all joined into one (incoming) flood.

casting-spear; 77 *franca*
Another word of great age, probably in frequent use in OE verse but preserved by chance chiefly in this late poem.... It probably meant a special kind of spear for throwing, javelin – but in verse according to habit it is used vaguely.

fatal; 91 *cald*
A pregnant word [literally 'cold'] connoting 'fatal'. Well used here with its double implication (1) applied to the actual water and (2) to the fatal crossing that marked turn of the battle and the beginning of disaster. OE verse use of words is full of subtleties of this sort for those who will observe.

For similar pregnant use of words cf. 96 *wælwulfas* which while describing vividly the Danes streaming like a pack of hungry wolves 'west over Panta', also connotes outlaws, enemies of all Christian men.

glory in battle; 104 *tir æt getohte*
Cf. *tir æt tohtan* (*Judith* 197). An example of how half-lines stuck in minds of poets. Here it does not fit too well. The usual word is *tohte* = battle array (drawn up?). The noun *getoht* only occurs here. There was none of the niggling schoolmaster's spirit about exact quotation.

the ravens went to and fro, and the eagle eager for carrion; 106–107 *Hremmas wundon / earn æses georn*
The ravens and the eagle (and also the wolf) were the traditional camp-followers, who became eager and active on the eve of battle in expectation of carrion. The crows and ravens probably remained actual enough. The purpose of their introduction was of course primarily to add to the grimness and the sense of gloom before the battle began. The raven as accompaniment of battle occurs in *Elene*, *Judith*, *Beowulf*, and *Brunanburh*.

The remarkable passage *Beowulf* 3024 is the only one where the poet really tunes his imagination on to these conventional trappings – The raven discussing his feed with the eagle is a direct link with the survival of this motive in the discussion of 'twa corbies' or the 'Three Ravens' of the ballads.

> Twa Corbies.
> *Ye'll sit on his white hause-bane*
> *And I'll pike out his bonny blue een,*
> *Wi' æ lock o' his gowden hair*
> *We'll theek our nest when it grows bare.*

shield received point; 110 *bord ord onfeng*
A kind of jingling phrase much liked – used to suggest echo as of repeated blows.

sister's son; 115 *swuster sunu*
The relationship was one of special import in Germanic lines and the especially close tie existing between uncle and sister's son is motive in several legends (notably *Finnsburg*).

There is however no reason to suspect that Wulfmær was not actually *swuster sunu* of Byrhtnoth, and this is a good

caution to that kind of criticism which would dismiss as falsi-
fication actual events and situations that happen to be [the]
same as familiar motives of legends. Things do not become
legendary unless they are common and poignant human
experiences first. The traditional affection of the relationship
(whether or not it be a last survival of matriarchy or not!) may
however have been the cause of the poet's special mention.

it is said; 117 *gehyrde ic*
Does not necessarily imply that the poet was not there, and is
versifying survivors' tales, and means no more than 'the tale
tells'. Note the subjunctive of report in *sloge* 117; it does *not*
imply any doubtfulness about Eadweard's deed.

southern; 134 *superne*
The 'Danes' may actually have often been found to have
weapons of costly sort plundered from France, Italy, Spain
– or acquired in Constantinople; but the word may also go
back to older heroic times when costly things were often so
denominated.

one of the Danish men; 149 *dreng*
A Scandinavian word. Here probably used wittingly as such.
This is the only occurrence in OE but it is found in ME.

Wulfmær the young; 155 *Wulfmær se geonga*
To distinguish him from an older *Wulfmær*, relative of Byrhtnoth, who fell earlier. *Hyse unweaxen* implies that he was only
in his teens. *Cniht* here has sense of *boy*.

All these words like *cniht* are tricky. Since young men
unmarried or not of full age are at once the most daring and
the most frequently in service they develop simultaneously in
different directions. The senses gallant warrior, blade – young

73

man, retainer, servant, boy, lad. *Cniht* in OE usually = boy....
Its elevation into the higher class is post OE and comes
through its sense of servant.

burnished; 163 *bruneccg*

With a glittering edge. A famous epithet. Cf. *brad ond brunecg*
of a *seax* (*Beowulf* 1546). *Brun* in sense shining (of weapons)
also occurs in *Judith*, *Beowulf*, and [Exeter Book] Riddle 17.

The sense dusky, dark, brown also occurs in verse, and is
the *only* one in prose of any period. This points (1) either to
the words being distinct (2) the other sense shining being conventional as applied to *metal*.

The word *brun* got from G[ermanic] into Romance hence
bruno; but it got there also in this sense of *bright* which occurs
frequently in *Song of Roland*.

In ME at least with its application to steel (and glass and
diamonds) it was understood as white-gleaming. It is suggested with probability that it is same as *brun* – brown, and
was first applied to swords of the bronze age, and becoming a
fixed part of the poetic vocabulary as applied to helms, swords,
spear-point, it changed its sense as these changed their metal
and appearance. Not an uncommon semantic development.

pale gleaming hilt; 166 *fealohilte*

Pale-hilted. *Fealu* in OE means pale, especially pale yellow (cf.
fallow deer), as of leaves going pale and golden. No connection with *fallow* of land. *Fealohilte* is nowhere else recorded.

steed; 189 *eoh*

The oldest word for horse. In OE it chiefly survived as *eo-* in
names like *Eomer*, being ousted (except in the language of
verse that preserved so many ancient words) by synonyms

such as *hors* (courser, runner); *mearh*, etc. Cf. *eored* = *eoh-rid*, a riding of horses.

in those very trappings of his, in which it was not right;
190 on þam gerædum þe hit riht ne wæs
(that he should appear) – because the Earl's horse was known, and probably specially caparisoned and richly harnessed: the explanation is found in 239 where it is seen that men took the figure of Godric galloping off on the well-known horse for Byrhtnoth and a panic ensued.

fit; 195 mæð
Lit[erally] measure, and is used in OE (and ME) for decent limits of moderation; practically here sense is 'than was at all decent' or creditable.

men of his house; 204 heorðgeneatas
Means personal retainers of a lord or king who lived in his hall, and sat at his board beside his hearth. Here no doubt it implies nothing more than the members of Byrhtnoth's own personal picked troops, the *heorðwerod* cf. 24. Though elements of the old conditions still survived. This is the word by which Beowulf describes himself and his companions when they arrive in Denmark. So a *heorðgeneat* was often in close touch (Cf. *Beowulf* 260–261). Beowulf was Hygelac's nephew.

Remember all those speeches that we have often spoken
at the drinking of mead; 212 Gemunon þa mæla þe we
oft æt meodo spræcon
Cf. *Beowulf* 2633 (Wiglaf speaks:) [Rendered thus in Tolkien's *Beowulf* 2208–13: 'I do not forget the time when, where we took our mead in the hall of revelry, we vowed to our master, who gave us these precious things, that we would repay him

for that raiment of warriors, the helmets and stout swords, if ever on him such need as this should fall.']

In addition to what is called the 'comitatus' motive, there is also the feeling that vows spoken in drink must be made good. The great classic example is the *Jomsvikings*, a band of celibate vikings (i.e. they occupied a permanent military fort where no women or children were) who held *Jomsburg* in N. Germany and became so powerful that they made kings. They put Swein Forkbeard on throne of Denmark. The most famous were Palnatoke, and Sigvaldi son of Strut-Harald. At the funeral drinking given by King Swein, there was fearful strong drink and enormous horns. [?They] had to drink cups of memory to the King's father, then to Christ, then to Michael, and then to Strut-Harald – and by that time they were in the mood for vows, and Earl Sigvaldi vowed he would invade Norway, and they all followed his vow.

The next morning the *Jomsvikings* felt very blue about it – they thought they had spoken 'big words enough'. But they set about it – and met with complete disaster in one of the most famous Scandinavian naval battles related in *Heimskringla* in which nearly 250 ships engaged. [Pencilled addition:] Note that we have a *convention* here, but a *living* one, for the commitments of comitatus loyalty were still fully genuine. They were still in personal touch.

forgetting not his desire for vengeance; 225 *fæhðe gemunde*
To bear in mind one's bitter hatred, the duty of vengeance, and so to show unsoftened valour.

shield wall; 242 *scyldburh*
This is probably the oldest term for what is also called in this

poem *wihaga* 102, *bordweall* 277. We gather what it was from
the gloss *testudo*...

Appears in OHG as *sciltburg* = testudo. ON has *skjaldborg*
as name of an ancient battle array. The classic description of
which is in *Harald's saga Hardrada* concerning the battle of
Stamford Bridge 1066. Generally it referred to bodies stand-
ing in close ranks shield touching shield – a formidable array
– so that for a single warrior with impetuous onslaught to
burst inside it as *Eadweard se langa* does is a feat. Cf. the
British Square in 'Fuzzy-Wuzzy' [1892 poem by Rudyard
Kipling].

249 *Sturmere*
The only place mentioned in poem. Most likely it = *Sturmer*
in Essex. And is a grain of evidence of the Essex origin of the
poem. Note that *Leofsunu* was *not* the author (he pretty plainly
perished) but that an Essex place-name is the only one to be
mentioned in 325 lines dealing with the fall of many noble
men might point to an Essex author.

men; 249 *hælæð*
It is interesting to note this old archaic pl[ural] surviving in
this late piece of verse.

a simple 'ceorl' [churl]; 256 *unorne ceorl*
Not a noble, or a man of noble-birth (*eorl*), though a free man
not bound by same feelings of aristocratic honour (according
at least to the notions of an aristocratic society) – but never-
theless laying down his life for loyalty. The poet probably felt
this as an especial testimony to the love Byrhtnoth inspired.
Dunnere would not have had to face the same obloquy on his
homecoming if he had departed after B's death.

unorne = humble, mean, of little value – of clothes poor, shabby. It is of obscure origin.

hostage; 265 *gysel*

We don't know what a 'hostage' was doing in B's retinue, especially one with an English name (whose father also was English). Note, however, that *on Norðhymbron* = Northumbria whether the Danes or English of that region are meant. In the confusion of those days when Northumbria was a separate kingdom (theoretically tributary to the W[est] S[axon] Kings) of course both English and Danes would often be in same army fighting against the W.S. forces. Nor does the English name prove pure English ancestry at this date – 100 years and more after the definite settlement of Scandinavians (turning to tillage, etc.) into Northumbria.

A parallel of the duty of the hostage to behave exactly as native member of the comitatus is provided in *Cynewulf and Cyneheard* where the British *gisel* in retinue of Cynewulf fights with the other king's men against the greater numbers brought by Cyneheard even though all are offered their lives.

Ecglaf's son, Æscferð; 267 *Ecglafes bearn... Æscferð*

Is oddly reminiscent of *Unferð Ecglafes sunu* in *Beowulf*.

271 *æfre embe stunde he sealde sume wunde*

The line is remarkable for complete substitution of rhyme for alliteration.

hung never back, unwearyingly he fought...; 281–2 *fus and forðgeorn feaht eornoste | Sibyrhtes broðor and swiðe mænig oþer*

The punctuation is difficult to decide on – we have a kind of 'flowing connexion'.

This is another verse in which rhyme is substituted for alliteration.

283 *cellod*

Meaning and etymology unknown. We have already seen the parallelisms that exist in *Battle of Maldon* with other surviving fragments of tenth-century verse. It can hardly be doubted that this passage and *sceolde cellod bord... Finnesburh* 29 are connected. Unfortunately both *Maldon* and *Finnesburh* survive only in eighteenth century transcripts. Whether the eighteenth century has corrupted one or both passages is difficult to determine.

[in battle slew Offa] that sea-pirate; 286 *þone sælidan*

Which? The one who had slain Byrhtnoth?

Note all the part from 184–286 is really devoted to a short episode in the battle: the flight of Godric, Godwine, Godwig, the rallying of Byrhtnoth's own personal following and their several speeches. The slaying of the *sælidan* is reserved, by *Offa* clearly the chief of B's following (cf. his proud words about the rest of the leavers at the war-council), until the end.

the kinsmen of Gadd; 287 *Gaddes mæg*

Clearly = Offa. We don't know more. *Mæg* in this way is used to relate a man to any notable ancestor – usually exclusively (but not always) his father. Gadd may have been uncle or grandfather.

an old retainer was he; 310 *se wæs eald geneat*

We have here another instance of old traditional situation and actual occurrence coinciding. We need not doubt that Byrht-wold *was* an *eald geneat*, and that he actually spoke memorable words not unlike the remarkable ones here enshrined. Yet it was traditional for the *eald geneat* to be relentless and daunt-less and 'speak winged words'.

With *eald geneat æsc acwehte* cf. the *eald æscwiga* of *Beowulf* 2042 whose place in the *Ingeld* story corresponds to that of the grim *Starkaðr* of Norse.

The old retainer is more jealous for the honour of the house than even the master is – but if this is a 'literary' situation it is only so because also it is a common one in reality.

> No one has yet doubted the authenticity of *Maldon* – why it has been thus neglected is difficult to say – but at least as sensible as some of the 'internal' criticisms of texts would be one that pointed how mythical it all is
>
> > the dear *swuster sunu* is the first to fall
>
> > all the characters make 'comitatus' speeches in the best 'epic' manner
>
> > the *eald geneat* comes in at the end preaching a courage of blank defiance of fate. In fact they might even say he was a fabrication of the poet, his name a mere variation of Byrhtnoth introduced to emphasize what the poet wished to present as B's character – but of course the two B's have a quite different character.

Each mind shall be the sterner...; 312–313 *Hige sceal þe heardra heorte þe cenre | mod sceal þe mare þe ure mægen lytlað*

These 2 lines are deservedly famous – in OE they are vigorous and sum up in curiously compact and forceful way the special quality of Northern heroism: unless you admit defeat you are not beaten, a cold grim and desperately hard creed, but a noble one, and not one that is at present in danger of being overpopularized and exaggerated. In fact read attentively one can hardly escape the impression that these lines are older and go back further than the texture of the context – a fact that Byrhtwold probably spoke these exact words because they were either proverbial or a familiar quotation.

PART THREE

The Tradition of Versification in Old English

with special reference to the *Battle of Maldon*
and its alliteration

[This fair copy manuscript of a wide-ranging lecture/
essay (*MS. Tolkien A 30/2*, fols. 35–38, 44–64) dates to
the late 1920s or early 1930s, when Tolkien was Rawlinson and Bosworth Professor of Anglo-Saxon at Pembroke College. I have found no precise means of dating
its composition or delivery, though it may have been part
of his repertoire during Oxford terms in 1928 and 1930,
where he is recorded lecturing on *The Battle of Maldon*. I
present the first 34 pages of the text here; the remaining
10 pages, a technical discussion of elements of *Maldon*'s
prosody in a series of notes labelled *a-f*, are found in
Appendix II. At points where Tolkien presents a series of
Old English quotations as examples of unusual scansion
or otherwise notable poetic features, I have in the interest of brevity omitted all but the first in the series, giving
only the line numbers for reference to those that follow.]

The Battle of Maldon is in a more hasty, or rather in a less
formal manner than the long poems that have survived
from an earlier age. Most of these are from their matter, or
their handling of it, seen to be the elaborated works of the
minstrel turned scholar (or the scholar turned minstrel)
rather than of the minstrel plain, the gleeman of a noble
lord. Such fragments as have survived of Old English verse

do not allow us clearly to distinguish separate prosodic varieties of composition, each with formally acknowledged difference of rule.* Yet to some degree recognized differences may have existed. It would be surprising, if it were otherwise, for the required conditions were present: learning, both Latin and vernacular, often going hand in hand; a lively interest in metres; a critical appreciation of native verse, and skill in its composition, among those who were also schooled in book-Latin. Sometimes all these things were found together in one man: such as Aldhelm, some of whose Latin has survived, and whose English verse, though it has not survived, had a long popularity and tradition which lasted for some hundreds of years.

Doubtless the native 'kinds' were not fully differentiated, and all varieties were interconnected in metrical rules, conventions, and poetical vocabulary. So that when Old English verse was used for different purposes, as divergent, say, as some of the Riddles are from *Beowulf*, it does not, in what has survived, show the formal metrical differentiation of, for example, the Latin epic hexameter and elegiac verse. But it still does not follow that its regulation was the same in all cases, and that the differences which do exist from poem to poem are simply to be ascribed to individual aberrations, to deficient skill, or to disorganization and decay. It does not follow that lines in *Maldon*, for instance, that do things never done in *Beowulf*, were necessarily 'bad lines' – to be marked with a dagger when not emended – made by a bungler or a man in a hurry.

---

* To this statement the 'Chronicle verses' (of various kinds) are to some extent an exception.

Still less necessarily does it follow that divergences between poems known to be late (such as *Brunanburh* and *Maldon*) and poems credibly conjectured to be 200 years or more older (such as *Beowulf*) are due simply to the passing of time – with the breaking of rules as its inevitable result. This would mean that metre and alliteration such as that of *Beowulf* could no longer be done in the tenth century, and metre like *Maldon* would have been scorned in the eighth. But neither of these beliefs are founded on proof, and both are probably unwarranted deductions from scanty material. It may seem in that case an odd chance that has so arranged that of poems in what might be called the freer manner the only examples should come from late in the tenth century. But reflection will show that this chance might very well be expected. It was probably a very odd chance that *Maldon* got written down at all, and a longer chance that a fragment of it then survived. But the odds are altogether against the few things (if any) of this kind that were written down in the earlier age surviving both the wrack and ruin of the North in the ninth century, and the disaster of 1066 and the overthrow of that relatively advanced and artistic English culture by the crude and semi-barbaric Normans, and finally the general havoc of the sixteenth. For the earlier age we depend upon later pious copies of casual survivors of serious and treasured books, brought south often in tattered condition. Cynewulf owes his survival probably to the rescue in the tenth century of a single manuscript. The Cædmonian poems are a sadly inefficient tenth-century collection of poems preserved we do not know how – though evidently they were found in older manuscripts much the worse for wear when the WS 'edition' was made.

Of all the effect that the many stirring events, major and minor, in which commanding or beloved men (such as Byrhtnoth) met victory or death, must have had upon poets and tale-tellers, only the brief episode of King Cynewulf and Cyneheard survives in the chronicles from the pre-Danish period – in the vernacular. Another odd chance – connected doubtless with the special interest of the Chronicle in the royal house of Wessex, just as the preservation in writing of *Maldon* was probably connected with Byrhtnoth's patronage of the church. The apparent relation, then, of regular (or rigid) metre to date is probably illusory, a natural accident. And if we look a little closer we shall see that even our extant fragments do not bear it out. Strict metre is found later than *Maldon*. In the same century we have pieces in strict metre in The Chronicle: *Brunanburh* in 937; *Eadmund and the Five Boroughs* in 941/2; the *Coronation of Eadgar* in 973; the *Death of Eadgar* in 975. Then remarkably in 1065 the *Death of Eadweard the Confessor*, written in technically good verse, with only one line that is not in strict form: *and se froda swa þeah befæste þæt rice*. This piece made seventy years and more after *Maldon* is in the compact epic metre, and precisely as 'superior' to it in that respect as is *Brunanburh* which lies half a century back on the other side. A hundred years after *Brunanburh* metre essentially the same as in *Beowulf* could be written. The similarity of the good Chronicle pieces to one another and their difference from *Maldon* is plainly a matter of purpose rather than of period. This has been observed by the fact that *Maldon* and *Brunanburh* are both concerned with battles. But this is really inessential. *Brunanburh* tells no story: it is a piece of Chronicle verse; the most elaborate and stirring certainly of these pieces, but still a piece for a place, a formal eulogy of the royal house upon accession, victory, or death.

In dealing with *Maldon*, then, we must be cautious of ascribing its so-called metrical 'defects' to change of metre, owing to decay of art or linguistic alteration. Metres change – or so we say: meaning that the practice of poets changes (not always from the decay of skill!). For 'metres' do not themselves change. A metre cannot change any more than a *triangle*. It is a shape, an abstract form. Once *consciously* recognized as a rule, or system of regulations – and this conscious recognition is an essential for the existence of metre in composer and audience – they can persist as long as poets find pleasure in them or have a purpose for them, and can be applied to linguistic material of different kinds at different times. All they need in a period of *oral* transmission is an unbroken succession of craftsmen. They can, of course, be simply lost or forgotten like the recipes or designs of any craft, if the national life and culture suffers some disastrous interruption. But this catastrophe, which did occur in the eleventh century, leaving the lines on Eadweard the Confessor as the last surviving work of the old court poetry, is quite another matter to the slow disintegration by time, which has so often been assumed. As if 'metre' was on a par with vowel-sounds, and suffered the same unconscious drift, which poets did not notice and were powerless to prevent! But linguistic change will never wholly explain metrical change; and when we move from period to period of one language (without a direct historical breach in cultural continuity) it has probably relatively small effect. The strict metre of *Beowulf* can be applied to current English; and there is no cogent *linguistic* reason why it should not have continued to be applied to English from Bede's day to our own.

The whole question is, in fact, more complicated than is usually observed. Metre is dependent on language: so much so that the slightest modification in the linguistic material affects it. In strictest analysis no two lines, written by the same poet on the same day in the same language, are identical. But this strict analysis is linguistic and phonetic not metrical. It assesses the differences between two lines; *metre abstracts their agreement*. Metre is indeed an abstraction, a pattern in itself devoid of colour, and so in a sense independent of its material: language. The same 'metre' applied to different material (different languages, or even different pieces of one language) can be compared to the same wallpaper design printed in different colours. Therefore the Latin hexameter is the same 'metre' as the Greek hexameter, though the result of the application of this metre to different material is not the same. But this difference, due to the great divergence in phonetic structures of Latin from Greek, is in fact precisely the same in kind (if greater in degree) as the difference between two hexameters in the same language, or between two poems in hexameters by different poets. Language can be said to have affected metre only when *for linguistic reasons* the rules have been modified: when things *not* previously allowed became permitted under what may be called linguistic pressure. Thus the stricter 'epic' type of Old English verse studiously avoids 'anacrusis' at the beginning of the second hemistich. This avoidance is a hall-mark of that variety of alliterative metre. But linguistic change has steadily reduced its convenience in natural phrasing: normal word-groups begin, more and more frequently as time goes on, with a weak syllable, as expressions like a host of warriors, for instance, replaces in normal older usage *hæleða mengo*, and so on. It is probable, then, that even if handed on in a continuous tradition, alliterative verse (when used for longer narrative poems, at any rate, in which a constant resistance to the leanings of the language is difficult) would have admitted 'anacrusis' before the second hemistich of at least one weak syllable. In other and stricter words, the poets would have *changed the metre* to fit different linguistic conditions; or in still more accurate words they would have adopted a different (though related) metre. For the old metre would still be there. It would not have been changed *by* linguistic change, or unconsciously! The avoidance of these 'anacruses' was originally deliberate. For though anacrusis was once easier to avoid, it still had to be avoided. Sequences of the type *a host of warriors* are common enough in the natural phrasing of even archaic Old English, and in the older verse are allowed in the first hemistich, as *ne ge] feah he þære fæhðe* (*Beowulf* l. 109). And at any date, from then until now, if and when a poet desired for technical or artistic reasons to avoid them, he could avoid them: and write the metre 'unchanged', defying the changes of the year with the simple weapon of purpose.

If we wish, then, to discover why the verse of one period differs in metrical practice (within a generally similar

kind) from that of another, there are many things to consider. Not only linguistic change. There are the individual
poets – in the history of English alliterative verse largely
lost – who by their own peculiar behaviour modified the
tradition that passed through them. One must at least
sometimes wish to know, even if one cannot find out
with certainty, by what methods the 'rules' were taught
or learned, and so handed on: what was the apprenticeship of poets and *scops*. And there is also, as a universal
condition, that inevitable change of taste and fashion, the
weariness of achievement that turns aside from progress
in one direction to wander in another, which contin-
ually overcomes all human art. But 200 years is not a
great while in artistic history, even when it is filled with
as much noise of battle and destruction as was that time
between, say, the death of Bede and the fall of Byrhtnoth. And the strain in English, severe as it was, was not
severe enough to break English tradition. Otherwise the
Battle of Maldon would never have been fought, and the
poem about it never written at all. That poem is linked in
almost every word with the elder poetry: quite as strongly
as *Brunanburh*, of which the derivative quality has often
been as much exaggerated as the 'freshness' of *Maldon*
has been misconceived. Yet of 'tradition' the easiest part to
hand on is metrical rule. A boy – *ex hypothesi* having some
bent for these things – can quickly grasp the scheme of
even fairly intricate rules, though he will still need much
schooling in the art of words before he can write even
derivative verse within that scheme, or employ the hered-
itary vocabulary and style of English poetry. And we have
seen that as a matter of fact verse much 'stricter' – that is

much closer to *Beowulf*, indeed metrically identical – was written both contemporarily with *Maldon*, and still two generations later.

Maldon then, as we have it, is probably to be regarded not as a piece of uncertain metrical skill, but as a survival by fortunate chance of the kind of less polished and compacted verse that was made to celebrate events while the news of them was still hot – and was accepted for what it was: a poem in a freer mode. A kind that was seldom committed to writing at all. In a sense it was a 'popular' kind – and for that very reason it is more in the direct line of ancestry to Middle English alliterative verse. The fact that we catch in it here and there the very accents of Middle English is probably as much an indication of its *kind* as of its *period*. *Beowulf* on the other hand is a scholarly and consciously artistic product of the union of minstrelsy and letters (and antiquarian lore), of the harp and the pen. However its maker worked – with quill or lead and scraps of parchment, or in his head – it has been highly wrought, and in metre, even down to its most minor details, has been polished to a remarkable degree still plainly apparent in the one damaged copy that survives. Economy and compactness, and unity of movement in metre are in it, as in verse generally and of all times, rather testimony to hard work than evidence of mere antiquity. In fact 'antiquity' has nothing to do with it, unless by accident of history – unless you can in history find some clear and special reason why at an older period a writer would *take trouble*, and at a later would not. Such reasons can sometimes be found in the history, moral or political, of a country. But in our case – within the so-called Old English period – the other explanation is far more probable: namely that the *kind* was intentionally different.

There do exist differences of *skill*, of course, among verse-writers, that appear even when the metrical intentions are the same. Even in a bad period some individual may be a fair craftsman; and even in a good period some can fall below the general standard. Good poets vary in this respect. But the 'strict' Old English metre was not overwhelmingly hard to write, *qua* metre. It is unlikely that the divergence of *Maldon* from strict metre is due simply to the fact that its maker tried to write strict metre and could not do it. He either did not know of the existence of strict metre, and knew only a laxer form, which he therefore used. Or else he knew of both and used the latter out of choice.* The former of these supposes a condition of things in tenth-century England which is not likely actually to have existed. For there is no question of the knowledge of the old stricter metre having everywhere perished: we know that it had not. We have therefore to suppose that it was only known in certain places or in certain groups of men. But in no place or group of men would it be more likely to be known than among the *heorðgeneatas* and *híred* of the great duke Byrhtnoth, akin

---

* I do not rule out the possibility of 'bad writing'.

When a metre is really hard or unnecessarily complex, or unsuitable to the purpose in hand a poet may eschew it and use an easier form, either out of consideration for his own inferior dexterity, or for a genuine artistic reason (and both motives may cohere). But the strict OE metre is not, especially not in Old English itself, hard or unnatural; it does not demand mere metrical gymnastics which interfere with ease of expression. The failure to produce it can thus only result from one of the alternatives proposed.

to the royal house, with lands in west and east, and men of Essex and Mercia (explicitly in the poem) among his following. Unless strict metre was indeed a monopoly of kings with crowns, it is precisely to the existence of such *hireds* that the preservation of noble minstrelsy must be attributed, and to their fall and ousting by lords of alien speech that its later decay must be ascribed.

It is, I think, necessary to examine in more specific detail the vague notion of 'poetic tradition' (especially as applied to words and forms before we scrutinize *Maldon* itself), to return to the idea that metrical forms decay or alter by an unconscious process analogous to, and indeed concomitant with, change in language. This finds superficial support in the fact that in early times verse has its life and descent mainly in *oral* tradition, and is so far in very similar case, it would seem, to language itself. But actually the only part of verse that is really on the linguistic plane is the language of it, phonetically speaking, the noises of which it is composed. When a man recites a piece of verse, the sounds he produces are 'traditional', and he is unaware or inattentive of their phonetic nature and method of production. But that which distinguishes this sound-sequence, among language in general, as 'verse' is on a different plane: it is a matter of which he is aware, and so are all of his audience whom it is worth considering at the moment. That is: the *metre* (and *diction*) are not abandoned to the realm of habit, though their use may be consecrated by 'tradition'. The same man may tie all his neckties with certain habitual motions of the hand which he has long ceased consciously to direct, but his selection of their colour is conscious, even if his choice may be determined by tradition, as of a black one for a funeral. Tradition, in fact, is better not confused with physical habit. The underlying assumption – to be seen in so many quasi-scientific analyses of verse-structure – is really that metre resides only in the individual example: as the colour of flowers or the shape of leaves is an inherent quality of the being of the species. Which would really mean that it is in fact perpetually forgotten, and reproduced only because the same language and same character successively throws out nearly identical forms. So the beech dies, and from the nut eventually the same-shaped leaves emerge. And as it is believed that in slow time the aberrations of the descendants will evolve a new beech with leaves of different form – are there not some that simulate the oak? – so in time the metre will dissolve and change. But if language is in some ways like this, verse is not. Here rather comes the woodman; and in the forest he cuts boughs and gathers flowers to weave a garland for his brows, to brighten his halls, or to adorn the temple of his gods. He chooses the shapes and colours from the riches of the wood, and what is not there he cannot take, but of such as there is he makes a design which resides in no plant or tree. (Though it may come from the Maker of all trees, and must forever remain arboreal.) That design can be copied as long as the wood is there; and imitated in other lands and woods; and it can be perceived, learned or taught, as a pleasing way of arranging leaves and flowers, as something imposed upon the components separable from the actual garlands of woodmen that have gone before us, even though contemplation of these may be the usual way of learning the pattern. And finally it is something we can impose upon ourselves, with our own individual tastes. We are not trees, and we do not write in 'metres' according solely to the unconscious leaflike unfolding of our native rhythms. We have each our native rhythms, like trees, but we have also 'tradition'. Both blend in poetry. But the trees make no poetry, because they do not conspire to teach the young how their grandsires shaped their leaves. (There is no conflict for them. They have a descent of the flesh only. They have not fallen.)

This parable is imperfect. For the garland, or in its more definite artistic form the painting, stays for a while. It too suffers time, and it may fade and its lines become blurred. But it has (with luck) a long life; and needs while it lasts no repetition. But a poem perishes even as it is being uttered. To live it must be preserved in memory and be after repeated. And men die quicker than pictures or monuments; and the time soon comes when the memory must pass into a different mind and the repetition to another mouth, or perish. And this whole prolongation of life, this 'tradition' can only normally be accomplished in and through the language, the 'habitual' element and the most changeable. If verse is compared to a picture it is a picture of which the primary pattern is made not by shade of colour but in line and balance, and yet in which these are represented solely by the boundaries of pieces of colour, and their correspondences.

And steadily as the line of tradition lengthens, the colour, the phonetic language changes. It is as if a picture with every view or exhibition changed slowly but inexorably from blue and silver to purple and gold, or what is worse that certain parts that once were alike diverge in colour, and others that were different grow alike. Such things may have happened to pictures, but they are not normal events in painting within those lengths of time that have seen considerable linguistic and phonetic change. It is true that much phonetic change can occur without necessarily disturbing metre: metre and diction on the whole stand the test of time better than the pure phonetics. But at any moment change may attack some phonetic feature that was used structurally, that was of metrical significance – the quality of a vowel or consonant in rhyme; the quantity of a syllable, its tone or emphasis. So linguistic change can be, and usually in the long run is, corrosive of metre.* What place does 'tradition' have in this conflict between art and change?

Metre and design are imposed upon language, even though they are ultimately derived by selection from it. But the fluid stuff of language will not take the impress permanently. What happens to this indurable coin as it passes from hand to hand? And in what way does the indurability affect the later moneyers who mint new pieces on the old models? And here we find a curious thing: the very people who seem to think of metre as a mere part of phonetic history, seem also nonetheless to ascribe powers to 'tradition' – at any rate in Old English which is our immediate concern – which it is unlikely to possess unless 'metre' is wholly independent of phonetics, and willing

---

* By which I mean of course not that metre changes but that to a man using metre in his head certain old lines will not scan. But what if the man reveres the old poets? Will he change the defective lines or the metre?

arbitrarily to defy them! What can tradition preserve, and what can it not?

I will anticipate here by saying at once that I think in general it can preserve *metre*, and some elements of *diction* including archaic *grammar* (which may become 'poetic' simply in the process of being preserved in verse after it has gone out of daily use), but cannot preserve *phonetic detail*. Not even a written tradition* can preserve memory of bygone pronunciation. Still less can an oral tradition do so. Because the only means of ascertaining pronunciation is in learning words, and it is precisely in this act of learning and using words that the changes occur; and yet the changes would not occur if they were actually appreciable at the moment, if they were made awarely and with observation. They pass below or beyond the attention of the normal man, the essential link in tradition; and he has seldom any ideas save the vaguest and most universal concerning linguistic change (such as that: tongues do like all else suffer alteration in time). And he usually regards his own familiar sounds as in some special way 'right'; while the 'rightness' of the metrical design depends, and must always depend, in metrical appreciation upon its agreement in the overwhelming main with this familiar 'right' way of uttering words.† The interesting and difficult

---

* Except as part of a specialist lore belonging to linguistic historians, which has no effect on poetic practice, not even if the linguistic historian takes to writing verse himself.

† I have of course my mind chiefly on Old English; and periods in which 'high language' used for verse is essentially only a cultivated variety of the daily tongue. The special efforts of *oral* tradition in certain cultural conditions, to maintain by sacred colleges, initiated orders, or priesthoods, the *right* pronunciation of obsolete or alien

question at once arises: what will happen, then, if a body of traditional verse composed in past generations is handed down through phonetic or other linguistic change which affects 'metre'? How do the 'archaisms' and conventions of verse arise; how does 'tradition' account for them or preserve them, and what is their relation to past *speech*?

The answers must vary at different times and under different conditions. But it is fairly clear, especially if we limit ourselves mainly to northern antiquity, that the primary condition is that there always was a tendency or a desire to differentiate the language of verse from that of daily speech – which was not essentially connected with 'archaism' as such. It was not antiquarian piety or philological curiosity but a belief and pleasure in '*poetic diction*'. With such a belief it is not difficult for forms not current in daily speech to become accepted (and by imitation traditional) in verse: it is a favourable atmosphere for the preservation of archaisms. But archaisms only of vocabulary and word-form: not of individual *sounds*. Let us glance at the 'words' before we further consider the sounds. In traditional verse there will in time come to be found a fairly large number of words, phrases, and constructions that are not used naturally in daily speech (unless by way of annotation, or the interjection of pieces of verse sentiment into one's colloquial utterances, a

---

tongues in the services of mysteries or religions, are not considered. We have not in Old English to do with conditions that obtained or obtain in the preservation of (or attempt to preserve) Sanskrit, Hebrew or Arabic – Latin itself, the sacred language of the West, had no such tradition. Its pronunciation was exposed to the constant influence of the vernacular.

habit once commoner than now, and which assisted in the preservation of 'poetic diction'). These will actually be in some cases poetic devices, made by poets for use in poetry, and so poetical from birth; and in others words that were entirely natural once upon a time, but which have since been replaced. But this distinction will not be of importance: being preserved now only in verse, both will have become poetical. Their preservation will indeed depend on their being found in memorized verse, or familiar phrases of verse; and their interpretation will depend on the *remembered contexts*. Archaic words that were once very frequently used will still be almost living, for the consensus of the many contexts in which they occur, each contributing to define or enlarge their sense (even when each is not severally consciously remembered), will act almost like real speech. But it will still be more limited than real speech, and such words will tend more and more to become stereotyped in use. Archaic words that were rarely used will have only a semblance of life: the contexts may fail to interpret them clearly; or they may even suggest false renderings.

We may thus get 'false archaisms' – which are really natural parallels, if sometimes more violent and arbitrary, to the shifts of meaning of living words in ordinary linguistic tradition, owing to the misleading suggestion of familiar contexts. We may also get, as in the language of everyday, the fossilizing of words, embedded in a phrase or expression from which they can no longer be removed. The learners of a traditional poetry are, when confronted by rare words or by *hapax legomena*, in much the same position as are later students, though they rely on memory, having no printed *Sprachschatz*. Imagine them confronted with *medostigge mæt mægþa hose* (*Beowulf* l. 924). This line contains two *hapax legomena.**

Now *medostig* gives us little difficulty. We can analyze it. Although we may feel it a little bold in its ellipsis, we are sufficiently familiar with the 'mead-hall', and the poetic way of putting things oddly, to feel certain that 'measured the mead-path' means 'paced the path towards the mead' (sc. mead hall). The Abingdon road is after all the road to Abingdon. And so if our fancy is tickled by this, we can repeat it with variations. We know all about the elements: *medo* and *stig* are both familiar words we can place in any required context, or replace with equivalents. But *mægþa hose* is different. The construction is plain enough. We know *mægþa*. But *hose* we do not. Our only clue is that it must, in such a context and construction, mean vaguely 'a company'. But this is not enough for free use. Imagine ourselves unequipped with any philology or knowledge of other Germanic tongues. Reference to Gothic or Old High German *hansa* was not available to the Old English poet. We do not then know (a) whether it is a general company word, or one suitable only to maidens, (b) what its form should be in any context when it is not used like this – in modern terms we do not know its gender or declension,

---

* Of course both may have occurred frequently in lost poems oral or written; they probably did. But the principle is the same. Oral tradition may preserve a greater body of verse than has survived in writing through the destructive centuries, but it cannot preserve everything everywhere, evenly and impartially. Language itself cannot. Learners of traditional verse must often have been confronted by problems exactly such as *Beo* 924 presents to us.

or what its form should be in any case other than the (comitative) dative. In all probability then, if we did not simply forget it because of its rarity, we should only dare to use it in precisely similar contexts, and in the fossilized expression *mægþa hose*. Old English and Old Norse verse offer many examples of this close repetition.

The case is similar with archaic forms. Some are general and their function, and equivalence with current forms, widely understood. Some are preserved only in certain phrases. We need not delay longer over this point; since language in general, and the language of our day as of any other, offers plenty of parallels. All know the use of *thou* and the corresponding verbal forms in *est*, and also *art*, *wert*, etc. They are preserved in the language of liturgy, and verse. We do not use them naturally, and may make mistakes in them, or find some now so odd that we avoid them (as *resistedst*), but they are available and preserved by 'tradition'. But we are not obliged to use them. Tradition, when not reinforced by writing and by formally taught grammar, may preserve archaic forms, but it *cannot dictate* their use. Our feeling that if one uses *thou art* in a poem, one should not later (without some special reason) relapse into *you are*, is a sophisticated one. Under Old English conditions one was rather always free to fill the prescribed metrical scheme with *current material* which according to contemporary use and pronunciation obeyed the rules; one could call on certain traditional forms to assist in metrical obedience or to give the flavour of 'poetry', according to convenience and taste. Of abstract lexicographical teaching, there is in Old English no record. It is doubtful whether learners ever heard statements in schoolmaster terms such as: '*hæleð* means "man" and if convenient you can use *hæleð* also as plural instead of *hæleðas*; compare *monaþ* and *monþas*.' Such abstracted teachings with regard to the element of *poetic diction* are not, at any rate, a necessary part of verse tradition. We do not really even now for all our dictionaries, grammars, and graduses, normally or necessarily acquire our poetic diction in this way. A way which marks the birth of philology – though that has naturally always been connected, especially in origin, with the study of traditional or archaic verse, and particularly with metre, whether in bardic lore or more recent philological investigations of Homeric and alliterative verse. Mnemonic lists of verse-words for *horse*, or *helm* or *man* and so forth may have existed. They existed in Old Norse, though to a certain extent their compilation is rather evidence of the decay of Skaldic craft than of its flourishing, due to antiquarian piety rather than practical poetical education.

Let us now return to the *metre* and the *sounds*. If you believe still that *metre* exists, or existed, only in particular examples of supposedly metrical composition, there is no difficulty. For then all such traditional stuff is simply metrical, and that is all you can say: you can neither approve nor criticize its 'metre' at particular points; for that requires some standard independent of the example. And even the attempt while listening to hear verse metrically – to find the relation to the norm of the pattern of lines that may seem aberrant – implies the belief in the existence of a pattern in the abstract. So if this is your belief all you can do in listening is to perceive vaguely a rhythm (as you might in engines, or the beat of hoofs, or birds' singing). And all you can do in emulation is to pour out words in an easy uncritical flow, and you can call it a rhythm if you wish. But that was certainly not the way Old English verse was written.

If you believe that *metre* was to the ancient poets a recipe independent of the pudding, then you have to consider how they got to know of the recipe; and also what happened when traditional verse, which in course of generations had changed its *pronunciation*, seemed here and there not to obey the recipe. As to the first question: We do not know. But it is probable that it was not in kind different from the way in which poets now acquire 'metres', though it may have been less haphazard; for a knowledge of such matters was probably more general and more generally esteemed. In other words, with the memorizing and hearing of verse there went doubtless also a certain amount of actual abstract description of the *rules*. Not organized, perhaps, or possessing a whole vocabulary of technical terms – though these possibly existed, as they did in Icelandic – but still a laying down of certain laws by which composition was to be directed, and verse judged. And certainly there existed the tacit assumption that there were 'rules', that verse could be regular or irregular, good or bad metrically.

It is unlikely that there was any definite 'profession' of minstrelsy, which one entered by apprenticeship and by which one after gained one's sole livelihood. Certainly there was no rigid bardic organization; and equally certainly one could acquire the mysteries of verse and make and recite it with approval without belonging to any craft. So it was in Norway and Iceland. Widsith, the imagined minstrel of the compiler of the necklace of legendary kings

and heroes in the Exeter Book, expresses his gratitude
for praise and substantial reward, and whither so he wandered he brought out his songs hoping for both. But he
was a king's ambassador, and his reward was princely, and
he gave it to his feudal lord Eadgils even as the warrior
Beowulf gave the rich gifts of Hrothgar to Hygelac; for
both received their inherited lands from their kings. Egill
Skallagrímsson was no less eager for reward and praise;
but he was a great warrior, of ancient house, a chieftain in
Iceland. He was certainly a *scop* or a *skáld*, but he was not
an initiated bard.*

Where then did he learn the rudiments? In his own
home. It was the custom in that house and the houses of
his father's friends that people should amuse themselves
over their drinking by reciting and making verses.† And
such also was the custom in ancient England. In Bede's
story Cædmon was very odd in being unable to make even
a moderate contribution to the general play. It was his
peculiar incompetence – so unusual that even a cowherd
was covered with shame because of it – that threw his later
miraculous inspiration into relief. A point rather missed
now, when the making-up of verse (and even the reciting
of it from memory) is so odd that it is rather versifying
that covers men with blushes.

In this fireside school both metre and diction could be
learned. The earliest efforts of Egill are reported. There
is no real ground for robbing him of their credit, even if

---

* But he belonged to a poetical family – whereof most Icelandic
poets owed their talent.
† *Það var þar haft ölteiti, að menn kváðu vísur* ['That was their way
there at ale-quaffings that men quoth staves'. *Egil's saga* xxxi].

we may believe the age at which he composed the difficult stanzas in 'court metre' – *Kominn emk til arna* (xxxi)
and *Síþögla gaf söglum* (xxxi) – to have been exaggerated in earliness. But the stanza *Þat mælti mín móðir* (xl)
attributed to him when about seven has the ring of truth.
In Iceland at any rate a boy of talent could master the out-
lines of *dróttkvætt*, a much more complicated metre than
the Old English epic verse, while still young and living in
his father's house. And the only later schooling in such
matters he got or needed, beyond doubtless listening,
and learning verse by heart, was the companionship and
rivalry with other *skálds* in the Norwegian court.

Now let us examine the second question and consider
the effect of old poems upon people who believed in metre
and knew it. Alliterative verse is specially useful in such an
enquiry. Certain of its features are so readily seizable that
it is impossible to imagine that they were not known to be
'rules' apart from poems – for example, at least it must be
admitted that everyone knew that such verse must 'alliterate', that is have a minimum of two words a line beginning
with the same consonant or with a vowel;* and that lines
that did not have this alliteration would not seem 'right'.
On the other hand this important feature of alliteration
is very liable to disturbance by phonetic change, and yet
is at the same time naturally intolerant of inaccuracy – of
anything in the least comparable to traditionally inaccurate end-rhymes, or to the preservation as eye rhymes

---

* But note this also implies a recognition both of the existence of
units or lines, and of their formation out of linked hemistichs! For it
is clear that both these minimum staves could not be lumped at one
end only of a line.

of the changed rhymes of past centuries. It is naturally intolerant of such things because in Old English verse it is used economically, and primarily not as an adornment but as a fundamental structural feature, linking the hemistichs into a compact line and often defining the way in which they are to be metrically analyzed: without it a line is more unacceptable than a couplet that totally fails to rhyme in heroic verse. But this essential* alliteration depends in principle upon a correspondence, readily recognized by the ear, between two sounds, often brief and not sonorous (like k or p), widely and yet variably spaced. Plainly inaccuracy will be much less tolerated than in end-rhyme, consisting of the recurrence of a sequence of sounds (including a vowel), normally at regular intervals, and often repeated many times. It would be interesting then to discover if we could what people, while alliterative verse was still current and living, made of old verse that phonetic change had damaged. One thing seems plain and that is that they could not keep up archaic pronunciation so as to preserve the lines. We are not dealing with traditional pronunciation of sacred books, with Vedas or Bibles; but with a general oral tradition, not devoted as far as we know to the reverent repetition of poems regarded as 'classics', but to the practice of the *ars poetica*, to the rules of verse and its adornment. And even the Latin of

---

* This can not without some training be fully appreciated now by English people long accustomed to end-rhymed or blank verse, and alliteration as an *adornment* (a function essentially different to its point in OE metre). Also our reading of OE verse is too careless usually to improve our metrical feeling. An Icelander can still readily detect (and object to) the absence of alliteration.

Scripture and liturgy were not in the early west preserved from phonetic change by a clerkly tradition of pronunciation. Latin pronunciation was *taught*, and exercised the schoolmasters a good deal; but it was in doubt, for it had been affected by the varying fortunes of sounds in different vernacular areas.

If a man who knows 'metre' is confronted with a poem in archaic language he is bound to come across lines that are no longer 'right'. He can then assume error, or if he is an acuter critic perceive that change has occurred. In either case in dealing with an oral poem he may change the line or passage so as to make it 'right' according to contemporary usage. This must often have occurred. In purely oral tradition it must have *normally* occurred. Though the loss of final *u* and *i* in certain conditions is a change that probably occurred long after the English came to England – it is normally ascribed indeed to the seventh century; and though such poems as *Beowulf*, and with perhaps more credibility other pieces such as *Widsith*, are widely held to contain embedded in them very ancient matter – still the critics look in vain for any certain case where a defective line occurs that only requires the restoration of this *u* or *i* to make it scan. Which is all the more remarkable in contrast with the loss of medial *h*. This is still in place in the earliest written document of English; but as a full consonantal sound it must have disappeared as well during the latter part of the eighth century, though the contraction of the resulting hiatus into one long syllable (that was not metrically appreciable as two) as in *giþiohan*>*geþio'an*>*geþeon*, must have taken place somewhat later. Now two things are here to be noted: (1) that

defective lines require the restoration of the older syllables as *man geþeon* in *Beowulf* are common in the older
poetry but (2) *their imitation in verse demonstrably written
in a period after the contraction was an accomplished colloquial
fact is nowhere to be seen.*

The deduction from this is, I think, that we are allowing our thought to be confused between oral and scribal
preservation. Writing down – probably a somewhat excep-
tional occurrence – has preserved for our perusal some
poems originally written in an early period. *But this was
no part of normal tradition.* Before ever our West-Saxonized
copies were made the poems were dead – as far as oral
tradition goes. We have no idea what they would have
become, if England had not been ravaged, and they had
descended by living repetition until say 950 or 1000 or
later – then to be collected, like the Elder Edda, by ama-
teurs of the past, on the verge of the Middle Age, and the
invasion of new modes.

Oral tradition contributed to their past – in the case of
such long formal poems as *Andreas* or *Beowulf*, provided
them with material – but however much traditional matter
and phraseology they used, their authors were scholars
who knew the art of verse, and such things as these (*Beowulf*, or *Andreas*) were never in this form oral, but made
and soon written down: their later history has been in the
scriptorium. Thus the upper limit for the composition of
Beowulf is after the loss of *u* and *i*; the lower before the
completing of the contraction of *þeo(h)an* > *þeon*. And
before that later date *Beowulf* must have been in writing,
mummified, safe from the corrosion of oral tradition, but
not from the worms of scribal editing. It is even likely

on various grounds – e.g. direct errors in West Saxoniza-
tion, due to misunderstanding of *archaic spelling*, present
in our text – that its scribal tradition has not been continuous, but has had a leap: transcription in the late OE
period from an MS made in the late eighth or early ninth.
There is indeed no need to assume more than two copies
between our text and the first writing down.

Now this gives extraordinary interest to the question
of alliteration on *g* in Old English verse – a question that
has not been given the attention it deserves. For here we
have another phonetic change (directly affecting alliteration not scansion this time) occurring later, right in the
full tide of Old English and in the very century of most
of our manuscripts, the tenth. Again I think we can show
that certain poems were composed and their texts written before that event, and not rehandled by oral tradition
after. But others were either made after that event or else
entirely remodelled after it. All the older poetry treats *g* of
all varieties as equivalent. This is still so in *Judith*. None of
the Chronicle poems do – not even those in strict metre
(937, 973, 975, 1065); and it can be shown that for the
author of *Maldon* also the front and back *g* were distinct
non-alliterating sounds.

I will take another point. If secondary 'stresses', certainly present in the archaic period, seem in the freer verse
of *Maldon* sometimes neglected, sometimes observed, this
is to be attributed rather to a general looseness of metrical
structure, and not (as I used to be taught) to the sporadic
use of archaistic half-lines preserved by tradition. Thus
the repetition of old poems, or parts of old poems, might
preserve, say, *ham siðian* 'to journey home' in memory,

and also reveal that this *had once been used to fill a hemistich*. But if it did not still fill a hemistich according to current pronunciation, it would not be used by people who knew the rules (and were trying to obey them). Either the phrase must be altered or added to so as to conform to the rules – very easy to do – or the rules must be altered to take in the example. The latter procedure is in Old English unlikely and in any case is nowhere seen clearly to have happened.* And still less likely in Anglo-Saxon conditions is it that 'tradition' would not only preserve *ham siðian* but would preserve in bardic lore knowledge that such cases were to be rectified by a pronunciation: *hám síðian* – if and when such a pronunciation had in fact ceased to be used. Since tenth century poets eschewed the alliteration of front and back *g* – although their non-equivalence would render 100 lines or more of *Beowulf* defective – because they did not in fact any longer in the current tongue alliterate, while in every point of scansion and diction their verse was encrustedly traditional, it seems plain that on this point, bygone sounds, a tradition had little to tell.

Now in *Maldon* we meet *Nu mæg cúnnian* 215, *a mæg gnórnian* 315 – so to be scanned according to the probable metrical interpretation of the lines in which they stand; and we have: *hám síðie* 251 which *must* be so interpreted.

---

* Since phonetic change in English has usually been in the direction of reducing the total quantity of words we should have in this way developed 'catalectic' metres. Such do occur in Icelandic and may have been generated or suggested in this way – though this is far from certain: sheer metrical experiment and invention is more likely. Other innovations are rather enlargements. Of enlarging catalectic forms, there is no certain trace in OE.

Compare *hám síðìan* in *Genesis* 2161. But this seems to conflict with such examples as *siðian mote* 177, which might appear to be a normal A-hemistich: *síðĭǎn móte*. But this cannot be explained by arguing that *hám síðìe* is 'traditional' and archaic, while *síðĭǎn móte* is a contemporary, and ready-made fresh A. You cannot call in the rules to explain the setting aside of traditional pronunciations in favour of the current, at the same time as you are calling on tradition to explain the non-current pronunciation in other cases. If tradition was strong enough to make *ham siðie* scan, it was strong enough to make *siðian mote* over-long. The reason is rather that *hám síðìe* was still so pronounced, and still a sufficient (if minimum) line-filling; whereas *síðìan móte* was a maximum line filling: Sievers A2,* seldom indeed found in the second hemistich in *Beowulf*, and is normally lightened in the first by double alliteration. The frequent use of these heavier groups in places where they are usually avoided in say, *Beowulf*, is one of the prosodic marks of this kind of freer verse. Other examples are *stiðlice clypode* 25b, 234b, 265b, and with anacrusis as well 72b. Related to this is the not infrequent occurrence of anacrusis in the second hemistich before A and E types: as 72 already cited, also A *mid gafole forgyldan* 32b, 242b, etc.; E *and ne forhtedon na* 21b, 49b. (Similarly A: 11, 55, 66, 68, 96 146, 189, 231, 240). Many of these could be emended by the omission of small unnecessary words, such as *his, to, mid*, or slight alteration as *ealle gemanodest* (for *hafast ealle gemanode*) 231; but not

---

* [The reference is to Eduard Sievers' classification based on types of alliterative half-lines. A2 is a variant of the 'falling' half line (/ x / x).]

so 21, 49, 96, 189, 240, 242. Whatever be the reason of these divergences* from strict verse (and others not yet dealt with) it is plain that it cannot be mere incompetence, or ignorance of the author. The great mass of the poem is in verse that, judged by *Beowulf* even, is regular, though it is less compact, and the style freer and less studied. It is going beyond the evidence therefore to say as Sievers does that the author of *Maldon* (grouped with those of *Solomon and Saturn* and the metrical Psalms!) is one who 'had only an imperfect command of the old rules'. This can only mean either he did not quite know what they were, or else he knew and could not conform in all cases. The latter alternative is absurd in the case of *Maldon*. The former almost equally so. Why he should have been unable to get knowledge of rules which others before and after him knew (and which Icelandic children acquired in the farmhouse) is difficult to say. And still more difficult is it to explain the enormous preponderance of lines that do conform – this could only be due to his poem being in the main a string of pure reminiscences or quotations of ancient verse: and that is in *Maldon* clearly not the case.

We must assume an intentional divergence of prosody. This looser freer kind, as I have said, may have all along existed precisely as a less studied form, and have continued to exist as a popular or ruder form after the French invasion, when the more formal modes perished, reappearing in the various ME varieties. It may, however, of

---

* Similar things are found in *Beowulf* as *weardode hwile* 105b, or anacrusis as in *swa wæter bebugeð*, 93b; *þa secg wisode* 402b, but even counting the cases where emendation is clear or probable the proportion is much smaller.

course have been derived from the *deliberate* acceptance by poets of the results of time and linguistic change upon the more compact phrasing of the older periods (which was the basis of the stricter verse). This action of change did not, as I have said, *alter metre* – it left the old kind intact for use if required. But it may have encouraged the development (*by poets*) of a freer looser kind, easier to fit to the normal wordier and more analytic syntax of the current speech, and so convenient for rapid and less studied composition. Thus *mid prasse bestodon* for *prasse* 68b; *hafast ealle gemanode* for *ealle gemanodest* 201b etc. But such elongated word-groups of course always existed: and whenever the freer type developed, it was rather by the purposefulness of craft than the compulsion of time. In Norse, a language that did not to the same extent or so quickly as English alter the compact brevity of older phrasing, we find new metres being devised by the deliberate selection and normalising of the maximum elements found in the older epic verse – the making of *málaháttr*. And in such intermediate and debatable cases as *Atlakviða* we have really a close parallel to the versification of *Maldon*. The action of time *is* seen in *Maldon*: but in the cases where it can clearly be detected it does not *alter the rules*, but allows the pattern to be filled with material which in the older stages of the language would not have fitted. That is quite a different thing. Thus *g* front and back had diverged and are no longer equated in alliteration. The gradation of stress in different parts of speech is also shifting. The strict subordination of one stress to the immediately preceding stress is probably making way for a more level stress, and so we *get Ælfhere and Máccus* with only alliteration on *M*.

The verb finite is no longer so generally subordinate to nouns, and is especially when it precedes its subject evidently at least equal to it in stress. So we have *STihte hi Byrhtnoth* 127, 139 (helped by crossed alliteration *geHLeop Eoh Ahte HLaford*), 240. Some compounds, especially those ending in *man* which was very frequently the second element in such words, are weakened: *brím-mèn* becomes *brímmen* and so we have *brimmen wodon* 295b, a variety that in *Beowulf* in the first hemistich would need double alliteration, and in the second would require lightening in the second main lift. But these are no breaches of the rules according to the purpose and reason of them.

In European verse, then, and in English verse we can have at once a tradition of *metre*, and at the same time connected but independently a tradition of actual *poems*. In this way already before the wide diffusion or practice of writing archaic words and forms might be preserved in old poems, and perpetuated in newer ones – for metrical convenience, and as poetic diction without special metrical reason. In this way in England at any rate could *not* be preserved the whole grammar and language of the past – this or anything like it only occurred when poems got *written*, and so left the stream of a tradition more or less. For the language of verse was no separate species and its life was bound up with the vernacular. This tradition could not preserve *obsolete* sounds. Obsolete equations (alliteration or rhyme) *when preserved in writing* may suggest to enquiry that an old identity has been disturbed; but without writing nothing is preserved but the fact that there is a misfit.

We do find, of course, in later times – especially after

the writing and reading of verse has become general, and even its composition with the aid of writing common – old collocations or equivalences, like *rhymes* maintained after they have in current pronunciation ceased to conform to the rules. Even so they are usually preserved for some metrical reason as the scarcity of rhymes to such useful words as *heaven, love*; though equivalence in traditional orthography may maintain some (such as *war* and *star*) which have no such excuse. But even so, even now with the spelling strongly impressed upon our minds, we do not usually in repeating older poetry 'mispronounce' *war* when we find it rhymed with *star*, nor *broad* to match *road*. And we could not do so if we had not a fixed spelling – at any rate we should not know which of an ill-fitting pair to alter.*

'Tradition' also is powerless by itself to enforce the use of archaic or poetical forms in all cases to the exclusion of current equivalents. It can only usually preserve them as optional. If certain words like *heaþu* are only found in OE in 'poetic' (originally dialectal) form, it is because they had no current equivalents in the language of the persons who made our copies. If we feel now any hesitation about mixing *thou* and *you*, or *eth* and *s* as in *sitteth* or *sits*, this is because of an actual book-knowledge of the past, and because of grammatical teaching. In oral tradition there is

---

* This preservation of past forms must be distinguished from the use in verse of *dialectal* variants, which in certain conditions may be available to a poet – as actual variants drawn from current language; such as *again* rhyming with *men* or *rain*. Of course with progress of time one of these dialects may cease to be current and the forms derived from it, being enshrined in poetry, become part of poetic diction.

no defence against new forms that have come to conform
to the rules. Only spelling protects us (if it is protection)
against rhymes such as *sword/fraud*; and even our spelling
boggles only about consonants,* it is too inured to dis-
crepancy in vowel sounds to object to *heart/part* or *warm/
storm*. In fact 'archaisms' preserved by tradition, affecting
sounds purely, and not vocabulary or grammar, are rare
and of small effect. To actual readers or hearers of verse,
or to makers of it that still use them, they are not 'archaisms', but parts of poetic usage or diction – 'licences':
conventionally permitted defects, not different from real
'licences' such as the inaccurate rhymes for *home* and
love which repose in the main upon the sheer scarcity of
good rhymes for these desirable words. They are either
tolerated as misfits – or else are made the starting point
of technical innovation: that is of alteration of the rules
so as to admit them. They do not preserve the noises of
by-gone days.† They cannot. Even if we pronounce *war*

---

* And not all of these: for a consonant has been lost in *night* as
much as in *heart*, but lost earlier; and the poets of a less pedantic
day had already rhymed *night/white* and so on too often for the
orthographically-minded to object. Also the missing consonant
was one that had wholly vanished. We have no longer (X), and even
spellings cannot preserve in general memory sounds that have been
entirely given up in normal speech.

† Similarly *wind* pronounced to rhyme with *dined*. This may
historically be derived from an older normal pronunciation in which
this word developed, as have *find, bind, blind,* and so forth. But its
preservation is due to the scarcity of rhymes to *ind* (a product of
linguistic history), which except in *wind* is found only in foreign
words or in fairly recent contractions: such as *sinned, pinned*. And
even here it is supported by the orthographical fact that *ind* usually
represents (aind). The poetic pronunciation is seldom used unless
compelled by rhyme.

to rectify the rhyme with *far, star* we shall still not recapture the actual sounds of *war, star* in the days when they did rhyme, for those sounds no longer exist in English. It would be amusing if we could recall a man of the late tenth-century and get him to read out some *Beowulf.* In the first line, and still more when he came to line 151 *gyddum geomore, þætte Grendel wan,* his own pronunciation would destroy alliteration. He would no longer make lines like those himself. Yet absence of alliteration would be disturbing. And they would alliterate to the eye. Now we have good reason to suppose that there was some reading of verse aloud by book at any rate in the later period; the books would hardly else have been made. And the *Saxonica poemata* that young Alfred learned to read were certainly not all (if any) contemporary West Saxon productions.* Was there any lore that taught readers what to do? I doubt it. Of course when back *g* had ceased to be a spirant initially, the spirant had not vanished from the language. It was frequent medially – a parallel in reverse to our initial preservation of initial *r* and loss before medial consonants. And we can usually (though it is surprising what difficulty even this comparatively easy exercise in phonetics presents to those not practised in or conscious of sound-making) reintroduce the *r* where it has been lost. But generally our natural method in such cases of false equation is to make one of the terms the same as the other (in our current phonetics) – if we try to rectify matters at all. An alliteration was, as I have said, under much more

---

* Though Alfred would have no difficulty in the matter of *g*. The two kinds of *g* still alliterated while he lived.

urgent compulsion to rectify. I fancy then that in the tenth century *Beowulf* was read so that one or the other of the current pronunciations of *g* was carried through the line. The first that occurred, probably, unless one was still a familiar word, and the other no longer current; or if there was phonetic difficulty. I imagine therefore that *Beowulf* l.1 was given a stop *g* in *geardagum*; while l.151 was given a stop *g* in *gyddum* (the absence of stave in *geomore* would not matter), because a (front) spirant was difficult in *Grendel*. But this would be quite artificial – the accidental product of a special preservation from antiquity by means of letters – and having nothing to do with normal tradition. It would be felt as quaint, even awkward and unpleasing, and would not be imitated in actual writing, any more than some of the odd rhymes and 'quaint' final *e*s of Chaucer are today – except for a joke or an exercise in ingenuity.

We will now consider in detail, because of their importance in an enquiry into OE verse tradition, the 'irregularities' of the prosody of *Maldon*. I shall pay chief attention to *alliteration*, for in this point *Maldon* is specially interesting, and to it we can apply with some confidence the principles derived from the above argument: that 'metre' is independent of phonetic change (though it may be affected by it with the consent of the poets); and that *current phonetics*, not an impossible tradition of lost sounds, nor even orthographic tradition, are reflected in poetic practice – above all in a poem in a free 'popular' and unstudied manner.

We are now dealing, nonetheless, with a *document*. However unstudied in composition the original poem may have been, the fragment of it that has survived has reached us only because written down, and copied after that. *Maldon* has therefore, since it left its author's mind and mouth, been exposed to the same dangers as other written works and more scholarly verses. Though it has had certainly a much shorter line of descent than many of them. Let the proven corruptions in *Brunanburh* – of which we have several copies – which must also have arisen in a comparatively short time, warn us that this short descent cannot be expected to have protected *Maldon* entirely. It plainly has not. Besides in this case the actual MS is lost and we have only a print made from a copy in the eighteenth century – a series which greatly increases the chance of errors and verbal disarrangements affecting metre. For the moment there is no need to go further than to point to the omission of *grimme* at the beginning of l.109, or the absence of the second hemistich of l.172, to see that all is not intact. All the same we will handle this question of corruption conservatively. Nearly all the 'irregularities' are capable of easy emendation; but some are *not*, and that should give us preliminary pause.

This question of corruption introduces a point with regard to 'tradition' that has not yet been considered. So far we have assumed the power of oral tradition to hand on verse intact, except for unobserved *phonetic* change in the actual words – with perhaps occasional consequential but deliberate changes to rectify any damage to metre that phonetic alteration may have caused. But though this simple process may occur in favourable circumstances, the machinery does not always work so well.

How did *Maldon*, for instance, reach a written form?

It may have come straight from the author. Some clerk reverencing the memory of Byrhtnoth may have heard (or heard of) the poem celebrating his last battle, and knowing its maker have taken pains to take it down. But it is more probable that it had already gained some currency, and passed through several mouths, before this happened. Now oral tradition of this sort even when running through only a few years (especially dealing with such 'topical' matter) is not only less reverent of verbal detail than is scribal, and far less than editorial, it is actually not capable of uniform fidelity – except in special cases, where special efforts are made (as in the case of liturgical or sacred poems). It is prone to error. Even in a period when through practice memories are acquisitive and tenacious, reciters, though they may be themselves makers and conversant with rules, suffer from minor lapses of memory, and moments of inattention to form – when the *meaning* survives rather than the exact *expression*. This is the common experience of all who attempt the learning and recitation of verse. It is precisely in such *gaps* that are likely to occur *substitutions of synonyms*, slight *disarrangement of words*, and hasty *patching* of the sense with a line or so that is barely metrical, or is in a different metrical manner. These stand out from the main texture, and so catch the eye or ear of the later enquirer whose attention is concentrated primarily on metre. But it is necessary that he should carefully consider what is the *proportion* of the really 'bad' lines – as judged by the general level – and how far they contain in themselves any *real difficulty* for a composer of the capacity revealed by the poem as whole. For example, outlandish names; translation (as for instance *in hoc signo vinces* which gives Cynewulf some trouble in *Elene*); the necessity of sticking fairly close to actual words in reporting speech (to which is allied the general difficulty of *oratio recta* and dialogue in verse, and especially alliterative verse), and so on.

If these 'bad' lines in a longish piece are very few* in proportion, and are all lines which present no inherent obstacles (such as could, for instance, be easily remedied by the substitution of a synonym, or a slight rearrangement of words) – it is a proper assumption for the *metrical historian*, if not for the textual editor, that in this small residuum he has the results of the imperfections of *repetition*. There are 325 lines in *Maldon*. Of these some as received definitely break essential rules – rules the poem normally obeys: namely 45, 75; 224, 271, 288. From this small number,† 75 is probably to be deducted (see below). This leaves *four* in which the cause or nature of the corruption (if any) is not obvious on ordinary editorial principles – which are thus for an editor's purpose 'genuine'. But I should feel inclined to ascribe precisely these four to imperfect repetition; and 271 I suspect to be a line not by the original author at all (but of this more below). None of them present any inherent difficulty at all. 45, 224, 288 are all easily emended or rewritten with words the author knew.

I have attributed imperfection to *repetition* not

---

* When we have deducted palpable mistakes ascribable to scribal *hubris* or tendencies.

† I leave aside the plainly defective 1, 109, 172, 183; and also 29, 32, 192 where as we shall see the breach of rule is only apparent, in spite of editorial daggers.

composition because, on principles already argued, such imperfections could only arise in composition by a less skilled man than this author, or by such a man in peculiar circumstances: namely when *extemporizing*. Now *extemporizing* produces exactly the same defects as appear in the 'bad patches' of *repetition*. Only, unless with a very skilled person, and one moreover practiced in the art of stringing conventional half-lines together, they will occur more often. The defects are the same because the process is: they occur when the meaning required is in mind but not its metrical expression, and the mind is not agile enough to find metrical words to fit in the brief time allowed. But *Maldon* is *not* an extemporized poem. It is or was too long. It is traditional in language, and it uses a good many 'stock phrases', but is plainly not just a string of these. Compare 975 *Death of Eadgar*: 7 *þa wearð eac adræfed, deormod hæleð / Oslac of earde ofer yða gewealc / ofer ganotes bæð, gamolfeax hæleð / wis 7 wordsnotor, ofer wætera geðring / ofer hwæles eðel, hama bereafod.* This is in strict metre – but it presents the kind of thing an extemporizer with any knowledge of traditional verse could go on doing as long as breath lasted, and without a single breach of rule. I could do it myself.

Extemporizing was, of course, practised. It was one of the ways the craft was learned, and skill in it exemplified. We hear of it wherever the making of vernacular verse was a widely esteemed and popular accomplishment – as in Iceland. But although some metrically intricate stanzas are (in literary texts) ascribed to impromptu utterance, even to repartee, we must make due deduction for touching up, literary invention, and exaggeration of the speed of composition. And in any case we must imagine that really extempore utterance in anything like a difficult metre was limited to very special persons, and in them to rarer occasions and *short stanzas*. It was not a normal method of composition, even in celebration of immediately topical events. Cædmon was not disgraced because, when the harp came to him, he could not then and there sing without any previous thought.* But he did not occupy his quiet in the cowshed with making anything up for later occasions. As now verse was naturally composed in privacy, in the watches of the night, and trotted out later at the symposium. To this natural method we have many references: not only in the case of Cynewulf, the polished (if unexciting) poet – who says 'At times I pondered and arranged my thought anxiously by night' (*Elene* 1239 ff.); but also in the case of the maker of a popular lay such as *Havelok*, whose author asks prayers for *him that haveth þe ryme maked / and þerfore fele nihtes waked*. To return again to the *skáld* Egill: he said in pretended anger of his friend Einarr Skalaglamm, another poet, whom he accused of wanting to get a poem out of him: 'Does he think I shall *sit up all night* on that account and write verse about his shield?' (lxxviii). Einarr himself in a strophe referring to his own famous poem *Vellekla* says: 'I wrote verse concerning the prince *meþan aþrer svofo*' (ibid).†

---

* Even after inspiration – his 'extempore' utterance as reported is *nine* lines long; his later works require thought. He studied his matter and brought out verse after 'rumination', as Bede tells us.

† [Ed. note: 'While others slept'.

'Made I the ale of Odin, / While others slept; for captain / That sits o'er earth, all eager / Wrought I – I'm sorry for it!' (201)]

The maker of *Maldon* (originally 400 lines long [pencilled above:] – probably more like 600) at the very least, we guess, and possibly much longer) did not extemporize this poem, and doubtless *fele nihtes waked*: at least this is a natural conclusion from its manner, subject, and general excellence.

Appendices

I

'OLD ENGLISH PROSODY'

[In 'The Tradition of Versification in Old English',
Tolkien alludes to the belief that '*metre* was to the ancient
poets a recipe independent of the pudding'. The excerpt
from 'Old English Prosody' (*MS. Tolkien A 30/2*, fols.
6–20) below extends this cookery metaphor in develop-
ing a 'recipe' for the craft of alliterative verse, one which
no doubt served Tolkien in the composition of new works
like *The Homecoming*. The text is numbered 1–29 and
dates to the early 1930s; the first lecture in a series on
Old English Prosody was delivered in the Examination
Schools at Oxford on 13 October 1932.]

This analysis is intended to be primarily *practical*. The
quarrels of metrists, which are more notorious than those
of theologians, are largely due to the failure to distinguish
clearly between an elaborate theory of rhythms, and an
analysis of the *content* of lines – no two lines in the same
metre being, of course, ever precisely identical from this
point of view – on the one hand, and a *recipe* on the other,
a pattern or scheme for the use of poets, a mould into

which they can pour, according to skill and taste, the infinitely varied matter of actual words.

It is the *recipe* we want – especially in Old English where it provides an essential and enormously valuable critical tool. It is the *recipe* which must exist, explicit or unconscious in both the mind of poet and audience (or student) if metrical skill or performance is to be appreciated more rationally than the vague pleasure found, say, by those ignorant of musical technique in listening to music. It is the *recipe* which must exist if a poet in fact is to write verse that is capable of any schematic analysis at all. The fact that OE verse is readily capable of such analysis is sufficient proof, even if Norse traditions did not exist to support us, that some such recipe did once, more or less explicit and teachable exist, even though all tradition and instruction in these matters (which was in all probability never committed to writing) has perished in England without trace.

The proof of the pudding is not only in the eating but in the making or at any rate reproduction. Only a *correct recipe* – though it may be expressed in words and in manner quite different from those of the original cook, and even perhaps unintelligible to him – will produce again the same pudding. Only using a recipe founded on Sievers' analysis – with modifications perhaps, but not fundamental alteration – can Old English verse be *written*: by which I mean can anyone who knows the OE verse language write new matter in it, which is not only a string of half-lines actually found in our records (this can be done without any metrical knowledge or theory at all!), and which does not only contain *some* lines of a pattern actually found, but also contains *no lines* which are *not* found.

This is sufficient to show that, however expressed or inculcated, the *recipe* of the poets in the classical period (say the eighth century) was the same as that expressed in our own odd way in our analysis.

We will therefore attempt our *recipe*. Do not let us be troubled by the cry that this is '*artificial*'. Of course it is! Verse is. Language is enormously complex and varied. It is impossible to find any two groups of words that are precisely equal from all points of view, that might be of metrical significance (which is all phonetic points of view, since 'metre' may take into account all points of phonetic analysis – length, stress, intonation, consonantal and vocalic structure, sequences of these, and so on; or it may be content to select from those, and leave the rest to taste). But 'prosody' – verse-planning – consists not in analyzing the intricacies of language, but in devising a pleasing pattern (more or less fitted to the tendencies of the language, no doubt) and fitting words to it. It is this interplay between the fluidity and variability of language, and the relative rigidity of the conscious and controlled pattern that constitutes at once the skill and the pleasure of verse-writing and verse-hearing.

Some *recipes* are extremely simple. This does not say that the verse written to them is necessarily simple or monotonous. It means that of the complexity of the phonetic structure of the medium the conscious and deliberate pattern has elected to regard only a few features or even one salient fact. In these cases the practice of a poet can hardly be fully understood from the bare recipe. From eggs flour butter and sugar very different puddings can be made according to various *recipes* (and various cooks). In such cases we are only content to say so and so is the 'metre', if we know for some reason or other that his simple pattern was all that the poet actually fully-consciously used, and that other important parts of his practice were due to less fully conscious processes, which we dub 'ear' or 'feeling' or instinct....

The OE recipe is nonetheless not one of the simpler ones, because its scheme took into consideration nearly all the phonetic facts of the language and bound them intricately together. Only vocalic structure (rhyme) was left 'unconsidered' – as part of the scheme – and handed over to the individual 'cook' as a seasoning to be employed according to need and taste.* OE recipe included *length of syllable* (time duration), *stress* (loudness) – of which at least three grades were consciously distinguished primary, subordinate, atomic – alternation in rhythmic pattern of line syllables, and *alliteration* on opening sounds (of loud syllables).

These were not isolated but indissolubly connected – *stress* and *length* were only considered *together*, and alliteration was infused in connexion with both, sometimes

---

* This of course no more means that OE poets disregarded vocalic structure than that Milton did, in spite of his remarks on rhyme. Alliteration is a most potent factor in non-alliterative poetry. The effect of *opening on the foam / of perilous seas in faery lands forlorn* (Keats 'Ode to a Nightingale') is mainly due to a pattern resembling but less schematic than the Welsh laws of cynghanedd. So vocal patterns play a large part in *Beowulf*. There are many obvious 'echoic' cases: *streamas wundon / sund wið sande* (212–13): thunder of surf; *mærne þeoden / hæleð hiofende, hlaford leofne* (3141–2) – *lamentation*.

dictated by them, sometimes colouring the words, and determining as it were the rhythm in doubtful cases. This function of alliteration is most important, and is frequently overlooked by critics who perceive the interconnexions of our artificially isolated types. But as a matter of fact enormous numbers of OE half-verses are susceptible of various analysis if the *alliteration* is unknown. Where the full line is set out and the alliteration known only in rare cases is there any doubt – except purely as to nomenclature.

We shall not expect a *simple recipe* then. But one thing must be noted – the poet's practice was founded solidly on the facts of natural, if formal and ceremonious, *speech*. In that he had an infallible guide in the classic period. It was only later when the established formulae and verses of the old poets became a convention at variance with the facts of speech that we get confusion and inconsistency....

For though deliberate employment of rhythm can be observed clearly in *Beowulf*, and changes in rhythm for different purposes, this is not part of the 'recipe', but a grace, colouring, or 'seasoning' specially employed by the poet....

OE verse is built entirely of blocks balanced against one another and a common rhythmic pattern was *not* achieved, nor aimed at. I will call its fundamental principle *weight*: this is length of syllable but not as measured in a machine...but as appreciated by the *ear*, and mind, easily influenced by concomitants *high tone, loudness, actual* importance in significance (for meaning), and *suggested* importance (the apparent importance given to words by form, portion in line, rhyme, alliteration, etc. – it is the constant attempt of OE to make actual and apparent importance coincide, but this is not of course with so tricky a thing as language always achievable). The *weight* of a verse element is in fact substantially *time duration*, but coloured by *loudness* (stress) and *significance*. OE verse is built like a wall or tower of solid chunks of more or less equivalent weight, each independent, but cemented by *alliteration*, piled course on course, or line on line. The basis is the weighty syllable and its normal concomitant the light syllable – this is the actual basis of the language. The simplest form of recipe for a *single line* is then this:

2 blocks (quite independent metrically) consisting each of 2 full elements or 'feet'. A foot is a *heavy* (weighty) syllable – a long and stressed (loud, significant) syllable – and a concomitant *light* syllable – a short and unstressed (quiet, insignificant) syllable. The cement is provided by the rule that the *first heavy* syllable of each block *must* begin with the same consonantal sound – which we will call, following the custom borrowed from Norse, *staves*.

II

THE TRADITION OF VERSIFICATION
IN OLD ENGLISH [CONTINUED]*

I will deal first with certain lines in which corruption is indubitable, whether its emendation is obvious or not. First of all 1 is defective because the MS is *capite mutilus.*† 109 has a word *grimme* omitted at the beginning (haplographically owing to its similarity to *grundene*). 172 has the second half missing owing to some accident (probably scribal).

More debatable lines may now be examined.

(a) Probably or certainly corrupt

1. 75: *wigan wigheardne, se wæs haten Wulfstan.* This is a case of the misplacement of the head-stave. There are *two* other apparent cases of this somewhat serious fault: 45 and 288. But whatever may be thought of these others, it is difficult to believe that 75 is recorded as it left the author. Its defect is so simply remedied, and the

---

* [For a description of this text, see note introducing Part Three of this volume.]

† [The beginning of the poem, as Tolkien notes in 'Beorhtnoth's Death', has been lost.]

APPENDIX II

corruption of so easy and frequent a kind. The author probably said: *Wulfstan haten*, which was still a current way of putting it, and so remained until much later. In which case we have in our text substitution of a wordier and more prosy equivalent. But in any case the received order is probably wrong (and may be due to transcription): the more natural order, even using the relatival expression, is *se Wulfstan wæs haten*. Compare: *An preost wes on leoden; Laʒamon wes ihoten, he wes Leouenaðes sone* [*Layamon's Brut*].

2. 7: *he let him þa of handon leofne fleogan.* This is defective in giving the stave to the weaker word (*let*) only in the first hemistich. The older language actually made finite verbs *in real speech* subordinate normally to concomitant nouns; and this fact was in consequence recognized in verse-making. It was *not* a metrical rule. The metrical rule was that of the two lifts in a half-line the loudest and most audible *must* bear the stave (the other might join in). The rule was obeyed if the most emphatic word did alliterate – the part of speech might vary in different languages or times, *without breach of metrical rule*. It is probable, both from the alliteration of later poems and from linguistic development, that the subordination of finite verbs became less and less marked in English, as a general rule. We thus find verbs taking the stave instead of nouns in various lines of *Maldon*. These are dealt with later. But in this line we have a verbal form and use that was specially weak. A preterite of this kind – especially in 'auxiliary' use before a governed infinitive – was often a mere 'dip' in the older verse, indicating pronunciation on a very low tone. *Letan* in this use is

moreover shown to have been weak by the development of forms with *shortened stem vowel* in ME (and other languages). We must then regard line 7 as defective. But it is at least likely that the ordinary prose word *handon* has been substituted for the poetical equivalent *folman*. A similar process is several times observed in *Beowulf*, e.g. 965 (*handgripe* MS for *mundgripe* shown by head-stave M.). That it has occurred here is further suggested by 108–9: *Hi leton þa of folman feolhearde speru*; and 150 *fleogan of folman*. The resulting crossed alliteration would according to the technique of *Maldon* suffice to correct the fact that the answer to the head-stave was still on a weak syllable. Compare *he gehleop þone eoh þe ahte his hlaford* 189 which is a parallel in reverse. Crossed-alliteration is a definite feature of *Maldon*. Clear cases of its normal form (abab) are 24, 63, 68, 98, 170, 255, 256, 320, and probably 285; of the form (abba) 159, 167, 189, 289. More fugitive cases of alliterative echo are 34, 75, 130, 151, 197, 262, 318.[*]

---

[*] The ending *um* of the dative (plural or singular) occurs 39 times correctly written in *Maldon*, including *handum* in its other two occurrences (4, 14). But *handon* even if the alteration occurred after the poem was written does not much support correction *folman*, since a clear case of dat. pl. *on* occurs in *mid leodon* 23 (beside 50). *on* also occurs in *hwilon* in reduced adv. use 271; and in 306, and after *on* in *on Denon* 129, 218, 266. Seven times in all. The latter cases, though the appearance of *on* is favoured by orthographic context, clearly indicate a phonetic change normally disregarded in spelling. This is a change of *um* > *on* (*o* for *u* being consequent on change of *m*). The regular *on* of the subjunctive in *Maldon* is primarily not a phonetic but a grammatical change due to assimilation of *en* to *on* beginning in the preterite present and modal verbs (so *sceoldon*, *Maldon* 19, 291, 307, *moston* 83, 263). *en* is maintained in pp. and such words as *þeoden.*

3. It is also difficult to believe that in 224: *he wæs ægþer min mæg and min hlaford*, we have precisely what was originally composed. The first hemistich is passable; the second must either be given a stress on *min* which is clean contrary to the natural emphasis and the opposition here of *mæg* and *hlaford*, or else neither scan nor alliterate. But it must be admitted that though (in a generally competent poem) corruption in such a line is highly likely – especially since it is so easy still to express precisely the required sense metrically and idiomatically that a native speaker of Anglo-Saxon can hardly have been metrically stumped – emendation, of the satisfactory kind that carries with it the explanation of the corruption, is not obvious.*

4. The absence of all alliteration in 183: *Ælfnoð and Wulmær begen lagon* has been generally recognized as due to corruption. The emendations possible are† *bewegen* 'slain' corrupted to *begen* under the influence of *begen* in the preceding line, which in itself makes *begen* in 183 suspect. Or mere omission of words: e.g *begen* (*on wæle*) *lagon*.

---

* Another case of prose-glossing is conceivable: e.g. (*min*) *hlaford* has replaced a poetical synonym beginning with *m*, as *mundbora*. Or the compound *heafod mæg*, a poetical equivalent of *mæg* may be concerned; but this probably requires us also to reshuffle the line to *min hlaford and min heafod mæg*. *Mundbora* occurs in the Chronicle poems of the tenth century especially in association with *Myrcna*.

† The weakness of the attractive emendation *bewegen* is that the word only occurs twice elsewhere, both in verse and both in sense 'cover'. Since *forwegen* 'slain' occurs actually in *Maldon* 228 it would probably be best to use this: in the special circumstances of the passage it would be almost equally likely to be corrupted into *begen*.

(b) Alliteration on 'weak' words

There remain some other lines in which the alliteration might be regarded as imperfect. The alliteration on a verb in preference to a noun has already been alluded to. Cases which are probably perfectly genuine are those already alluded to above: 128 *Hogode to wige* (contrast *Yfeles hogode* 133); 242; 127; 240; 189. The last as pointed out above is assisted by crossed alliteration. These may be parsed not simply as freer technique, but actually as conforming to the rules owing to the increase of *verbal* stress – especially as in four of these five cases when it preceded its subject. But in *wénde þæs formóni man þa he on méare rád* 239 the emphasis on *moni* naturally lifts it above the other words.*

The occasional stressing of a verb is actually found in the older poetry, and examples are also seen in the Chronicle poems (in strict metre): e.g. *þæs þe us Secgað bec* (*Brunanburh*); *beFæste þæt rice* (*E. The Confessor*). Probably sufficiently alliterated is 282 *Sibyrhtes broðor and swiðe mænig oþer*. Thus interpreted† it is in scansion passable according to the system of *Maldon*, with elongated types

---

* The first hemistich of this line is of a freer or more casual type – but does not break the rules: the language is colloquial not formal. *Man* is quite weak and subordinate; *moni man* is a colloquial substitute for the missing weak or pronominal form of *monig*, and is metrically equivalent to (/ u). The prefix *for* – it is not really a separate adverb – in the sense 'too' or 'very' (like Latin *per*) is sometimes stressed, usually not. Compare the variation with prefix *un-*, and the variable stress of our 'too': *that is* too *many* or *that is too* many. *Forswið, forswiðe* in *Wonders of Creation* 26, and Psalm 84 respectively, and *forwel* Psalm 131 are shown by alliteration or scansion to have unstressed *for. forheardne* in *Maldon* 156 has stressed *for*. These are the only verse examples.

† For the stress on *swiðe* cf. l. 115.

discussed above. But here we have probably the adjunct of rhyme. This will be discussed below with reference to line 271.

(c) Misplaced Head-stave

More serious are breaches of the rule with regard to the place of the head-stave in the second hemistich. A cardinal rule of the older practice (Norse and English) was that the head-stave must be borne by the first stressed syllable (or lift) of the second hemistich. This is not broken in good verse, because it is essential to the structure of the verse. Disregard of this rule alters its character altogether. In *Maldon* we find nonetheless (beside the case of 75 dismissed above)

> *gehyrst þu, sælida, hwæt þis folc segeð* 45
> *raðe wearð æt hilde Offa forheawen* 288

Editorially we must probably retain these, since their emendation is not obvious, and *Maldon* to an editor is primarily the fragment as received. But for the metrical historian they may be regarded as corrupt. They are the only clear cases of the non-alliteration of the first lift in the second hemistich: and this is a bad fault. To attribute them to the capable author of the poem is difficult – unless his poem was extemporized, and never revised; both are less likely than corruption through repetition. They seem to me fairly clear cases of damage by repetition (if not by scribe) according to the process considered above. For in both cases there is no difficulty whatever in expressing the thought metrically, even with words that are employed

elsewhere in the fragment; still less with OE material generally. An Anglo-Saxon would need hardly a minute's
thought each if we asked him now to put these lines right.

In 45 the poet had *flotan* (72, 227), *lidman* (99, 164),
leode (23, 50) not to mention other synonyms for *sælida* or
folc to work with; or a trifling rearrangement *hwæt segeð þis
folc*, which while not so good would have been a natural
order to him, and sufficient to his technique. Of course on
the normal *editorial* principles we are naturally reluctant
to replace a good *poetical* word like *sælida*, because it has
become an almost axiomatic assumption (certainly having
some support in MSS of the older poetry) that scribes
usually substituted prose-words if they substituted anything. But we have not only scribes to reckon with.* Here
we have probably *reciters* contemporary with the poet who
knew *sælida* just as well as he.

In 288 we cannot well reshuffle the order. Placing *Offa*
at the end would rectify metre, but is quite unnatural. If
there is corruption, it is due either (a) to Offa having crept
in unwanted from 286, causing dislocation and possibly
word-loss: a very likely event in *oral repetition*; or (b) to *æt
hilde* having been substituted (e.g. after *forheawen æt hilde*
223) for some other words, not necessarily expressing
the same idea: again a very likely event in repetition. In
the former case we can compare 113–5: If *Wulmær* had
crept in on 115, ousting *he* 114 and *swiðe* 115 the alliteration would have been destroyed. In the latter we may

---

* If the corruption is scribal it probably resides in *gehyrst*: i.e.
A prose-substitution for (*ge*)*frigest*, a poetical word: 'dost thou
enquire?' The resulting crossed alliteration being then closely
parallel to 189 and the proposed emendation of line 7.

suppose a word for battle, or weapons, has been altered; or other suitable sense, beginning with a vowel has been altered: e.g. *mid ecgum* (cf. *ecg* 60 and *mid billum* 114).*

(d) Minor irregularities of alliteration

The poem as received has several other lines that present minor irregularities of alliteration. The following contain, probably, not so much contravention of old rules, as evidence for a slight shift in language.

Thus: 308 *unwáclìce wæpna neotan* shows an unstressed *un-* in contrast with, say, *únwàclìcne* (*Beowulf* 3138). But *un* (originally in pre-Germanic an unstressed form) showed a natural tendency to lose its stress, or to vary it (as still). Unstressed use is found even in the older verse: cf. *unMúrnlìce madmas dæleþ* (*Beo.* 1756) contrasted with *eteð angenga Únmùrnlìce* 449.

But 57 is more unusual: *ùnbefóhtene nu ge þus feor hider*. The alliteration only of Lift 2 is quite in order, granted that Lift 2 is not of inferior emphasis to Lift 1. The treatment of *un*, rhythmically separated by a weak syllable from the stressed stem, as not superior to it is less common. Contrast *unforcuð* 51. But this treatment is probably in accordance with actual language, and due to the alteration of the strict subordination of the second of two stressed syllables which generally obtained in the older language. As of similar kind therefore are to be

---

* Note *raðe* 288 does not certify that the alliteration was on *h*. Both *hr* and *r* are proved by alliteration in OE verse, and both forms are etymologically distinct. In *Maldon* the written form is only *raðe* which occurs also in 164, where it does not share in the alliteration.

regarded 298 *þurstanes Sunu wið þas Secgas feaht*; and 80
Ælfere and Maccus Modige twegen. Though easily improved
by transposing of *sunu* and *Maccus* they are probably genuine. Similar also are 266 *he wæs on Norðhymbron heardes
cynnes* and 242 *scyldburh tobrocen abreoðe his angin*. The
latter is easily re-written with transposition (though the
resulting type is not good) or substitution of the synonyms
bordhaga, bordhreoða (neither of which however occur else
in *Maldon*). The former is improved by the form *Norðan-
hymbrum* (in which case it becomes parallel to 80, 298).
But though neither are strictly regular according to the
old language, they are probably genuine: 266 as testimony
to an actual pronunciation *norþhymbre* (cf. Northumber-
land); 242 to a special emphasis on *tobrocen*. In that case
266a is not C (a type which when genuinely present is
naturally intolerant of alliteration only on the second lift)
but A with a slight lift and even alliteration on *he*. The *b* in
burh assists in smoothing 242.*

(e) Rhyme

Without any alliteration is 271: *æfre embe stunde he sealde
sume wunde; st* and *s* do not alliterate. This is also remarkable in having rhyme – which thus appears, for the first
time in a poem generally in competent alliterative verse,
as a substitute for alliteration, not as a mere ornament.
Rhyme as an adornment both *aðalhending* and *skothending*
is found in all OE verse, either inside the hemistich in the

---

* Alliteration of Lift 2 neglecting a preceding adjective is also seen in
ealra þæra Wynna 174; and *þæt þu minum gaste* 176. But these can be
parallelled in older verse, and *min, þin* were variably treated.

jingles of which *Maldon* 110 (*bord ord onfeng*) is an example; or at the end of hemistichs as in *Byrhtnoð maþelode bord hafenode* 42 (and similarly 309);* or in more complex and purposeful (but extra-metrical) arrangements, as in *streamas wundon / sund wið sande* (*Beo.* 212–213). In 282 we have a case in which rhyme is nearly victorious.†

Yet I do not believe that 271 actually proceeds from the author. It is isolated, and detachable (and weak in effect). It seems to me that it has slipped in from a different style – that of more popular recitations, or semi-metrical '*gieddas*', which must have been going on, though we have scant record of them in Old English. In such as we have – the *giedd* passages in the Chronicle, which though treated scribally as distinct from narrative 'prose', are not alliterative verse, and in some cases marked only by an antithetical phrase-group style similar to that of verse‡ – it is noticeable that grouping by rhyme is specially frequent with *sume*. As in 1036 CD Ælfred Æþeling: *sume hi man wið feo sealde, sume hreowlice acwealde*, etc.

But of course rhyme, which from time immemorial

---

* Cf. also *eorl to þam ceorle* 132. Compare *ceorlum 7 eorlum* Menolog. (Abingdon Chronicle l.31)

† The only parallel to rhyme usurping the function of alliteration that I can point to is rather a remote one. The type of half-line in OE that consists of *three* stressed words (usually arranged as D or E types) is common. There are 70 examples in *Beowulf* in the first hemistich, and in every case they have *double* alliteration, except only in 1422 *flod blode weol*, where clearly rhyme is used for the same effect in lightening the weight. Cf. *flod blod gewod* (*Exodus* 463). A late example of rhyme with alliteration is seen in Chron. 1067 Margaret (lines of irregular scansion but all alliterated): *mid lichomlicre heortan on þisan life sceortan*.

‡ Such as 959 DE *Character of Eadgar*.

linked words like *ceorl* and *eorl* as much as alliteration linked others like *þeoden* and *þegn*, and which teased the ears of the poets, even without the example of the hymns of the church, and the example of late Latin known to clerks, cannot be excluded from the knowledge of the author of *Maldon*. It is really a question of style and suitability: and of this we are perhaps not now the best judges. It has no longer in the vernacular the novelty that might lead even a competent alliterative poet into an error of taste, for the pleasure of showing off a jingle. In all that has been said above, the fact has not been denied that taste can falter or fail – though the rules abide.

(f) Minor defects of scansion

The presence of elongated types has been alluded to above in dealing with *siðian mote, þa flotan stodon gearowe* and similar half-lines. Also anacrusis in the second hemistich. These have been attributed to an actual *difference* of rules to those obtaining in certain kinds of composition: *Maldon* though a 'good' poem, in which we scrutinize suspiciously defects in the cardinal matter of *alliteration,* is in a freer looser scansion, not necessarily (though possibly) a development more recent in time than say the scansion of *Beowulf*. In general it has resemblances to *málaháttr*. And it certainly is akin to the development of ME, in which overweighting, especially of the first-half, destroyed the original balance of the older structure. We see in *Maldon* increasing weight in the beginnings of types that open with 'dips', B and C. Thus *he hæfde god geþanc* 13; 50; 93; 195; 212, etc. But such things are, of course, found in all the older verse: it is only a question of proportion and general

effect.* The general effect in *Maldon* is of less compactness, greater wordiness. We therefore note with curiosity
examples that seem to fall *below minimum*. Examples of
over-lightness are: *folc and foldan feallan sceolon* 54; 264;
299. 270 also is notable.

---

* But we do not get except occasionally and probably accidentally
three staves in the first half – which is nearly as destructive of the
proper character of the metre as two staves in the second. *Wodon þa
wælwulfas* 96 is the only clear example and is probably casual and
hardly felt – but is the sort of germ from which the ME overweighting
and triple-alliteration might develop. Not unconsciously! But by
choice of poets – who nonetheless must be judged to have lost the
taste for and perception of the structure of the old economy.

III

ALLITERATION ON 'G' IN *THE BATTLE OF MALDON*

[In 'The Tradition of Versification', Tolkien notes that 'the question of alliteration on *g* in Old English verse... has not been given the attention it deserves'. The essay from which the following excerpt is drawn shows Tolkien vigorously pursuing the question. Four versions of this work, probably dating again to the early 1930s, are found in Bodleian *MS. Tolkien A 30/2*. The excerpt given here (version beginning fol. 155) once more demonstrates his esteem for the anonymous *Maldon* poet.]

Line 192: *Godwine and Godwig guþe ne gymdon* was treated by Sievers (*Altgerm. Metrik* p. 41) as possessing four staves, and an example of 'mangelhaft technik'. It is actually nothing of the kind, but an interesting testimony that at the date when the poem was written front and back *g* had diverged so far that the ear refused to recognize them as alliterating consonants. Verse was written by ear not letter; but while orthography, the main lines of which were a product of seventh- and eighth- century scholarship, remained conservative, the actual sounds of the language had changed very greatly.

In the line quoted the first three initial *g*s, the stave-bearers, are back *g*s. A similar arrangement occurs also in line 32: *þæt ge þisne garræs mid gafole forgyldon*. This fragmentary poem contains 325 lines, and in these two cases alone is there any (apparent) infraction of the cardinal rule of Old English verse: that the second half-line must contain only one stave. This by itself is sufficient to suggest that in these two lines the rule was not broken *to the ear*. The front *g* had probably at this period ceased to be spirantal, and was already the semi-vowel, as in our *yet*; while the back *g* had certainly become (as it certainly had not yet in the archaic period) a stop, as in our *good*. The suggestion becomes certainty if the remainder of the lines are examined. There are 23 lines in all that alliterate on *g*. In every case the alliteration is between 2 (or 3) back *g*s, or between 2 (or 3) front *g*s; in no case is the alliteration left solely to a mere letter-correspondence between 2 written *g*s representing different sounds. Only one doubtful case occurs: 100 *þær ongean gramum gearowe stodon* ... But the author probably, in fact certainly, regarded his line as alliterating *ongean* / *gearowe* with *gramum* not participating – its spelling with a similar letter is accidental....

The only apparent exception thus disappears; and we have, in the only poem by a man who had a command of his metre and its technique that has survived from the latter age of Old English, clear evidence of the careful distinction in verse between the two *g*s. We may deduce then that by whatever process the rules and practice of alliterative verse was handed down, it was by ear and not book....

Old English verse technique as we know it though working on an inherited metre, manner, and vocabulary, is English and not primitive Germanic. It is a product of the seventh and eighth centuries, to the language of which period it must have been extraordinarily true – observing with nicety most departments of phonetic structure consonantal and vocalic, stress and tone. The English had good ears, and though their verse is the most interesting and remarkable evidence of this, their orthography – for its period an achievement – should not be forgotten. Both were products of the same golden age. But it is of the nature of orthography to fossilize, and of metre to change for good or ill, so we already see the two at variance before the end of the Old English period, before metre sank to stuttering, and good spelling was overthrown by bad French to its lasting confusion.

IV

AN EARLY *HOMECOMING* IN RHYME

[As has been noted, one of the remarkable features of the early drafts of Tolkien's verse drama is that the dialogue rhymes rather than alliterates. The text given below is that of Version *D* (Bodleian *MS. Tolkien 5*, fols. 16–22)]

THE HOME-COMING OF BEORHTNOTH BEORHTHELM'S SON

The scene throughout is in darkness. Two voices are heard: those of *Totta* the gleeman's son, a youth, and *Tudda* an old servant of the duke *Beorhtnoth*, who have been sent by the Abbot of Ely to the battlefield not far from Maldon. There the abbot and some monks are waiting to bear Beorhtnoth's body to Ely.

Darkness. Noise of a man moving about & breathing heavily.

TOTTA

A! Who is there? You, Tudda! I had thought
That, God!, 'twas one of them. An hour I've sought

here, waiting for you, groping among the slain,
alone.

TUDDA

  Nigh here is where he should have lain;
but the moon is sunk.

   [He lets a light shine from a dark-lantern.]

TOTTA

    No, no! cover that light!

    [An owl hoots.]

Hish! What was that?

TUDDA

    Come, come, lad! What's your fright?

   [He covers the light.]

Help me to lift 'em, and spare breath! Less talk!
What do you think? That their ghosts so soon would walk?
Or wolves wander out of lays of Goths and Huns
in Essex here? Nay! Not two-legged ones
neither – they'll not come here to-night, to prowl
round corpses stripped near naked! 'Twas an owl!

TOTTA

Curse owls! I'm glad you're here at last. But 'fright'!
I'm not afraid – though I don't like the night,
with all these dead unburied. 'Tis like the shade
of heathen hell. Where has our master laid
his mighty head, so proud and old, to-night –
so cold and strange, when soul has taken flight?

TUDDA

Look where they're thickest lad! As here. Come, see!

[Opens the light.]

Here Wulfmær lies! And close to his lord he'll be.

TOTTA

Which one is that?

TUDDA

Which? Why, they both are here,
tumbled together: the man he held most dear –
not far from kin will lie his sister-son –
and Wulfstan's boy, too.

TOTTA

He that used to run
so swift, and swim? It seems an hour ago.

TUDDA

And Ælfnoth by him too.

TOTTA

And rightly so,
they were never far apart.

TUDDA

Nor far from him!
A plague on this lamplight, and my eyes are dim.
But it was here they made their last stout stand,
I'll warrant we find the old man near at hand.

TOTTA

Poor lads! While men with beards and tried blades ran,

the young boys died, God's pity! Curse the man
who left them to it. Young Ælfwine, look!

TUDDA

He was a stout one. *His* knees never shook.
Proud heart, proud tongue, like Offa.

TOTTA

                      There were some
took Offa's words with scowls, and wished him dumb–
they cut too nigh – or so I'm told, that day
at counsel of the lords. As old songs say:
''Tis shame to take the ring and drink the mead,
and leave the giver of the gift at need'.
But days are worsened. I wish that I'd been here,
not left with the baggage like a thrall in rear.
I loved him as much as they. A plain churl
may prove more tough when tested than an earl
that traces kin to Woden and old kings!

TUDDA

You talk! Your time'll come, my lad. Then things
will look less easy. Iron has a bitter taste,
and swords are cruel. If you'd ever faced
the yell of spears, now thanking God you'd be
you're neither dead nor shamed. Come stand by me!

*[A pause in which they struggle with bodies. The lamp is
stood open on the ground.]*

Now! Heave him off! 'Tis only a cursed Dane,
great hulking heathen.

TOTTA

Shutter that light again!
I can't abide his eyes. They glare so grim –
like Grendel's in the moon. Look! There's a limb,
like three men's legs!

TUDDA

Peace! It's the master! Yes,
that's him – the longest in this land, I guess.

TOTTA

His head was o'er the crowns of heathen kings!
Here lies he now at last, who dealt the rings
like princes in old songs. He's gone to God,
Beorhtnoth our lord.

TUDDA

And the ground about is trod
to bloody mire.

TOTTA

His sword is over here!
You know it, Tudda: with the golden hilts.

TUDDA

I fear
'tis well the moon's gone. Little have they left
of what we knew.

TOTTA

Woe! Tudda, they have reft
his head, and with their axes mangled him!
And the body – a! is battle then so grim?

TUDDA

Yes, yes – that's war. But we must make a shift
to bear what's left. Hold here! Now come! You lift!

TOTTA

None the less dear shall be this flesh and bone,
though foes have marred it. Now for ever moan

> The Saxon and the English men
> From Mercian wood to Eastern fen.
> The wall is fallen. Women weep.
> Build high the mound his bones to keep!
> And there shall lie his helm and sword,
> And golden rings be laid in hoard.
> For of the friends of men was he
> The first and best from sea to sea;
> To folk most fair, to kin most kind,
> And ever shall be held in mind
> While from the sea there riseth sun;
> Glory he loved and glory won!

TUDDA

Come on! No dirges yet! 'Twill be the part
of Ely monks, with luck. Now for the cart!
Hey, steady there. Keep step with me. Now slow!
Dead men drag earthward. Hey, look where you go!
What is it?

TOTTA

> Look! There goes one, see? No, two!
Two men! Or shadow-walkers foul of hue,
bowed, with long arms!

TUDDA

Quick! Put him down! And wait,
and keep your tongue.

[He puts the lamp out.]

*[A pause in which the noise of stealthy steps is heard approaching.
Tudda raises his voice.]*

Hi, there! You're over late
to join the fight. But I can give you some
if that is what you want.

[To Totta in hoarse whisper.]

Look out! They come!

[There is a noise of scuffling.]

[Tudda loudly] Go on! Trip him!

[A blow and a shriek.]

TOTTA

A! there, that settles you!
(Crying aloud) Heaven be praised, Tudda! I've run him
through, with master's sword! Quicker than he thought he
found the best thing left to plunder on this ground!

TUDDA

No need. That sword was made for better fare.
A fist and boot was quite enough to scare
the likes of them. There's dead enough about.
When you have killed a Dane, begin to shout!
There's plenty of them near, and by the Rood
I hate 'em, heathen or sprinkled, devil's brood.

TOTTA

> Then hurry! There may be more at hand. Away!
> We'll have the pirate pack on us.

TUDDA

> Nay, nay!
> These were no Northmen! What should they come for?
> They're all in Ipswich now, and drink to Thor.
> These are corpse-strippers, native carrion-crows
> of waste and fen. They have no friends nor foes,
> save want and hunger. One has found the gear
> of dead men sharper than he thought. D'you hear?
> Come on!

TOTTA

> God help us, and these wretched days
> when men lie unavenged, and wolvish ways
> folk take for need, to pill like carrion-bird
> and plunder their own. All hallows! There's a third
> in the shadows yonder!

TUDDA

> Let be. He will not wait.
> That sort will fight no odds, early nor late.
> They sneak in when all's over. Up again!
> Steady once more.

TOTTA

> Say, Tudda, where's the wain?
> I wish we were by it! Come now, more this way:
> we're walking near the brink. Look out, I say.
> We'll fall into Panta. And the tide is high.

157

TUDDA

We're at the causeway – and the wain's hard by.
There then – the first step of the journey's done.
By Edmund's head! our lord's not light with none!

[A pause. Sound of men slowly walking, and panting again.]

TUDDA

The wain at last! I wish that I could drink
his funeral ale right now upon the brink
near where he died! Good beer he gave; not thin,
but sweet and strong... ...
　　　　　　　　... ... How came they thus to win
across the causeway, think you? There's little sign
here of hard fight, and yet just here the brine
should have been choked with them. But by the bank
there's only one there lying.

TOTTA

　　　　　　　　They've him to thank,
alas! Or so men say now in the town.
Too bold, too proud! But he is fallen down,
made fool of by great heart. So we'll not chide.
He let them cross to taste his sword – and died:
the last of the true sons of men of old
that sailed the seas, as songs and books have told,
from Angel in the East, and under helm
upon war's anvil smote the Welsh, and realm
here in this isle they founded, long ago.
Now from the North again the winds do blow!

TUDDA

And poor men catch it in the neck, today

as long ago; whatever the songs may say,
perish all Vikings! Poor men robbed of land
they loved, must die and dung it. Lend a hand!
And then our task is done. Now up! That's right!
Cover him over with that cloth. It should be white,
but it must do for now. The monks now wait
in Maldon with their abbot, and we're late.
Get in! And weep or pray, my lad. I'll drive.

TOTTA

God guard our going, and grant that we arrive!

[A silence in which a rumbling & creaking of wheels is heard.]

Where first tonight? Lord! How these wheels do creak!...
...Hey, Tudda! Tudda! Speak! Why don't you speak?

TUDDA

(Heavily) Tonight? To Maldon; then to Ely, lad,
with monks and all, slow; and the road is bad.
Without a rest. Did you think to get to bed?

TOTTA

'Tis a long road.

TUDDA

   But a short one for the dead.
Creaking won't break his rest. Lie by, and sleep!

[To the horses.]

Gee up! boys. You've been fed. No need to creep.
Good stable have the monks. Don't heed the sound.
None now will try to steal what we have found.

[The creaking and rumbling and sound of hoofs continues for some time. Lights glimmer in the distance. There is a faint sound of chanting borne on the wind.]

TOTTA *(Drowsing half in dream.)*

Ay! Candles and singing, and the holy Mass
in Ely, ere he's buried. And days will pass,
and men – and women weep in Angelcynn –
and new days follow...... and his tomb begin
to fade, and all his kith pass out of ken.
The candles gutter in the wind. Like men.
They soon go out, the candles in the dark.
Come smite the flint, and strike a spark!
A flame – a light – a fire that won't go out!
A yes, I hear them. Good words those, and stout!

A solemn voice says slowly:

*Hige sceal þe heardra, heorte þe cenre,
mod sceal þe mare þe ure mægen lytlað.*

TOTTA

Well said the scop! And that won't be forgot
for many an age... an age...an age... *[sleeps]*

[The cart bumps and he starts.]

What?

Hey, rattle, rattle, bump! Tudda, I say,
No sleep! The roads are rough in Æthelred's day.

[Complete dark and silence for a while.]

[Voices chanting low and faintly, but slowly and with distinct words.]

AN EARLY *HOMECOMING* IN RHYME

Dirige, Domine, in conspectu tuo viam meam.
Introibo in domum tuam: adorabo ad templum sanctum
tuum in timore tuo.

A voice (not of Tudda or Totta).

Sadly they sing, the monks of Ely isle!
Row lads, row! Let us listen here a while.

[The chanting slowly grows louder and clearer.]

Dirige, Domine, in conspectu tuo viam meam.
Introibo in domum tuam: adorabo ad templum sanctum
tuum in timore tuo.
Domine deduc me in justitia tua: propter inimicos meos
dirige in conspectu tuo viam meam.
Gloria Patri et Filio et Spiritui Sancto: sicut erat in
principio et nunc, et semper, et in saecula saeculorum.
Dirige, Domine, in conspectu tuo viam meam.

[The chanting fades into silence.]

V

NOTEWORTHY DEVELOPMENTS IN THE DRAFTS OF *THE HOMECOMING*

[*The Homecoming* underwent many fascinating twists and turns over its twenty-year development from early scraps of rhyming dialogue to the finely tuned alliterative drama of more than 350 lines. I document some of the most remarkable of these revisions below, focusing chiefly on those that bear on the drama's most critical themes and episodes. Each of the four sections opens with my own commentary before tracking significant changes in the manuscripts (following Honegger's classification and the Bodleian pagination).]

THE SCUFFLE

What would a drama, let alone a 'sequel' to the Battle of Maldon, be without some clash of arms? Yet in the ironic mode of *The Homecoming*, the thrill of battle even for Totta is short lived, giving way to confusion, embarrassment, and shame as his opponents are shown to be not ravaging viking warriors but local wretches and petty thieves – more Gollum than Grendel. The drafts show Tolkien keen to perfect the discovery of Beorhtnoth's sword, its ignoble use, and the inspiration for his 'double-barrelled joke' in *Maldon*.

Version *a*:

This early fragment begins with Pudda (> Totta): 'Come, hurry. There may be more. Let's get away / or have the pirate pack on us' (*ToI* 106). Presumably the scuffle has already occurred off-stage, though many elements of the final work are already present: Pudda mistakes the figures for Northmen and is corrected by Tibba (> Tída); a third scavenger is later spotted, though any threat he poses is dismissed by Tibba.

Version A:

In the Bodleian draft marked earliest copy, it is Tudda (Tída) who discovers Beorhtnoth's famous blade: 'His sword is over here'. When Totta detects the intruders, Tudda springs immediately to action, encouraging his companion to take up arms: 'Quick! put him down! Out sword, out! / –well find one then, there are many left about' (*MS. Tolkien 5*, fols. 2–3).

Tudda's reaction to the outcome is also markedly different at this point: 'Heaven be praised, Totta, I've run mine through. / Yours dead? With the gold sword? I am glad he found / the best thing left to plunder on this ground'. As in the final version, Tudda corrects Totta's mistaken impression that their opponents were Northmen, identifying them as 'corpse-strippers'.

Version B:

Scene setting in faint pencil is added after Tudda's call to arms, suggesting a real threat from the approaching scavengers: 'Two men come up with swords in the gloom from behind' (fols. 6–7).

Version C:

Tudda here actually takes up Beorhtnoth's sword in the fray: 'Heaven be praised, Totta. I've run mine through / with master's sword!' (fol. 10v).

Version D:

See Appendix IV. The action, while still told in rhyme, begins to resemble its final form. Totta comes into his role as the sword-finder; Tudda calls out a warning, and encourages his companion initially; Totta crows over his deed and inherits the grim joke; Tudda chides his use of the sword.

Version E:

Tudda chides Totta in this first alliterative rendering of the drama: 'You're wild Totta. Now wipe it clean, / that blade was made for better uses' (fol. 26).

Version H:

'Ha! Take it then! Tída! Hona la! / I've slain this one! He'll slink no more: / a sword he found sooner than he hoped for; / but it turned and bit him. It's a trove indeed, / the best plunder that the battle left us!' (fol. 68v).

AT THE CAUSEWAY

When, in the published text, an exhausted Tída and Totta arrive at the causeway, carrying the headless body of their master back, as it were, to the scene of the crime, they pause for reflection. Of all the episodes in the drama, this is the one most plainly connected to the argument developed in 'Ofermod' – and it might plausibly be said to have inspired the essay as much as *Maldon* itself has done. A puzzled Totta wonders why the English appear to have made no use of this strategic position; Tída responds with the morning's gossip from town and censure of Beorhtnoth's fatal error. Totta does not deny the charge, though he does respond with a song echoing the Chronicle verse *Brunanburh* and commemorating Beorhtnoth's fall. While some allusion to this deadly turning point in the battle is present from early on, the scene undergoes much development in the drafts.

Version α:

Pudda (> Totta) inquires: 'How did they win / Over the bridge, think you? There's little sign / here of bitter fight. And yet here the brine / Should have been choked with 'em, but on the planks / There's only one lying. Tibba (> Tída) responds only: 'Well, God have thanks' (107).

Version C:

Here Tudda (> Tída) puts the question, and Totta bears the bad news: 'They've him to thank / Alas! Or so men say now in the town. / Too bold, too proud! But he is fallen down, / made fool of by great heart. So we'll not chide. /

He let them cross to taste his sword – and died, / the last of the true sons of men of old / that sailed the seas, as songs and books have told...' (fol. 11).

Version E:

Totta again muses: 'It's strange to me / how they came across this causeway here / or forced the passage without fierce battle / but there are few tokens of fighting here'. Tudda replies: 'Alas Totta the lord was to blame / or so in Maldon this morning men were saying / Too bold too proud – but he is beaten down / and his pride cheated, so we'll praise not chide / He let them cross the causeway so keen was he / to follow his fathers in fearless deeds / and hand to hand to hew foemen / and give minstrels matter for mighty songs. / Doom he dared and died for it' (fol. 27).

Version H:

Here the text reaches essentially final form, with Tída's criticism ('needlessly noble', etc.) via corrections in blue ink (fol. 69v).

TOTTA'S DREAM

In perhaps the most iconic episode in the drama, Totta drowses in the waggon after his harrowing journey, with only Beorhtnoth's 'body for bolster' on the long road to Ely Abbey. He dreams first of his lord's funeral mass, but the lights of the candles at mass are soon quenched by a grim and dark vision of the inexorable movement of time. The scene shifts in the second half of his dream, moving not forward but back in time, and in the lighted hall he joins in the song, chanting Beorhtwold's creed of desperate courage, the most famous lines (not yet written) in all OE verse. The two phases of Totta's dream emerge already in the early drafts, but Tolkien appears to struggle in deciding whether and how to integrate Beorhtwold's iconic speech.

Version A:

Totta, drowsing in the cart, begins to describe a vision of Beorhtnoth's burial and the slow ruin of time: 'Ay! Candles and singing and the holy Mass / in Ely, ere he's buried. And days will pass, / and men; and women weep in Angelcynn; / and new days follow, and his tomb begin / to fade, and his kith....Candles soon go out!...' The dream vision then shifts: 'Ay! yes, I hear them – good the words, and stout. / Well said the scop! That will not be forgot / for many an age...an age...an age....' It is jarred, then, by much the same bump as in the final version: 'What? / Hey, rattle, bump! Tudda, I say, / no sleep! The roads are rough in Æthelred's day!' (fol. 4).

Version C:

The good, stout words only implied in the earlier drafts are inserted explicitly here, with a 'solemn voice' calling within the dream: '*Hige sceal þe heardra, heorte þe cenre, mod sceal þe mare þe ure mægen lytlað*' (fol. 12).

Version D:

See Appendix IV. The call for a light provides a transition between the two dream phases.

Version E:

In this first alliterative draft, the vision reaches near final form, with the OE expression rendered in modern English and extended through three additional lines: 'Let heart be prouder, harder be purpose, / more stern the will, as our strength weakens! / Mind shall not falter nor mood waver; / though doom shall come and dark conquer, / and our flesh fail us, fire we kindle!' (fol. 29).

While in the final text it is Totta who chants the lines (albeit in the dream), Tolkien considered other presentations. A crossed-out ascription here clarifies: 'A deep voice neither of Totta nor Tudda says slowly'. A pencilled note suggests that Tolkien was still undecided whether to quote the lines from the old poem or render them in Totta's voice. The rendering of the heroic code is again different: 'Mind shall not falter nor mood waver, / will shall not weaken, though the world tremble / and our flesh fail us. The fire liveth'. Totta then adds: 'Well sung and said. The song is fading, / but while the world remains the word shall linger!' (fol. 30).

Version K:

Tolkien appears to have tinkered with Totta's rendering of these lines to the very end: even here, in the typescript sent to the printers, marginal corrections were needed to bring it to the published form (fol. 111).

THE MALDON POET

The suggestion – and its attendant implications – that the young Torhthelm, 'son of a minstrel', may very well represent Tolkien's imagined *Maldon* poet in the making is sometimes missed. Just as a first-time reader of *The Lord of the Rings*, ravenous for heroic romance but having little appetite for prologue and appendices, might pay little attention to the conceit of the Red Book of Westmarch, and to the role that Bilbo, Frodo, and Sam have in the very making of the tale, so too might the reader of *The Homecoming* be forgiven for seeing it as no more than a dramatic coda to the battle. While some hint of Totta's role as poet remains in the final text, Tolkien dabbled with but ultimately abandoned an explicit designation of Totta as the future poet.

Version C:

In the introductory scene setting, Tolkien describes Totta as 'a young stable-lad' though this is crossed out and replaced by 'the gleeman's son, a young man' (fol. 9).

Version D:

At the top left margin of the opening page of the verse drama, in faint pencil, Tolkien writes: 'Totta is of course imagined later to have made the extant poem, from hearsay' (fol. 16). This is the last extant copy in rhyme.

Version H:

'For the purposes of this modern poem, it is suggested that Torhthelm (Totta) afterwards, when the duke's body has been brought to its long home at Ely, composes the poem, *The Battle of Maldon*: made up from his own knowledge, from survivors' reports, and from imagination and epic tradition – the last surviving fragment of ancient

English heroic minstrelsy' (fol. 63v). This passage, along with other draft material under construction for the introductory note 'Beorhtnoth's Death', is crossed out.

In another draft of 'Beorhtnoth's Death', a footnote to Tolkien's remark on the originality of Beorhtwold's famous expression reads: 'It is here supposed that Totta afterwards becomes the author of the poem the fragment of which survives. It is based (on this theory) partly on survivors' reports, partly on imagination and epic tradition' (fol. 65v). The entire page is crossed out.

VI
PROOFING THE PUDDING: *THE HOMECOMING* IN DIALOGUE WITH THE LEGENDARIUM

'without the high and noble the simple and vulgar is utterly mean; and without the simple and ordinary the noble and heroic is meaningless'. – J.R.R. Tolkien, in a letter to Milton Waldman

It is to be hoped that readers of this volume will find in *The Battle of Maldon* and *The Homecoming of Beorhtnoth* something of that 'intrinsic' interest that Tolkien describes in his introductory notes to the OE poem. But many will inevitably and understandably also wish to explore their 'accidental' significance, to ask what light Tolkien's engagements with *Maldon* shed on *The Lord of the Rings* and the legendarium. As it is, I think, a good question, and I count myself squarely among such readers, I devote these final pages to its exploration.

Tolkien himself hinted that such an inquiry might yield fruit. In a 1964 letter to Anne Barrett at Houghton Mifflin, he claims to have 'had for some time vaguely thought of the reprint together of three things that ... really do flow together', naming *The Homecoming* alongside '*Beowulf*: The Monsters and the Critics' and 'On Fairy-stories' – two texts often considered the critical bedrock of any significant study of Tolkien's work (*Letters* 350). More pointedly still, he once remarked to Rayner Unwin that *The Homecoming* is 'very germane to the general division of sympathy exhibited in *The Lord of the Rings*' (*Chronology* 696).

While *The Homecoming* may not have properly monopolized Tolkien's attention for years at a time, its long and robust development – which almost uncannily tracks the publication of his major works of fiction – also suggests that it was seldom very far from his mind. Early drafts share the page with artwork and verses like 'Errantry' (see Introduction). It is difficult to say how far work on *The Homecoming* had advanced in the early 1930s, but it had certainly begun long before 1937, when both *The Hobbit* and E.V. Gordon's edition of *The Battle of Maldon* were published. Fifteen years later, Tolkien would write euphorically to a Mr Burns of two forthcoming publications:

> I also heard both that a dramatic dialogue in real alliterative verse (of various styles) on chivalry and common sense (in the mouths of two fictitious Anglo-Saxons) had been accepted; and more remarkable, a 'romance' of at least 500,000 words: exhilaration. (*Chronology* 414)

When *The Homecoming* finally appeared in the 1953 volume of *Essays and Studies*, it was followed just nine months later by *The Fellowship of the Ring* in July 1954.

On the surface of things, *The Homecoming* would seem

an odd prelude to *The Lord of the Rings*, even if it is, in barest summary, a story of two ordinary companions traveling through a nightmarish landscape on a difficult quest. While such surface-level analysis has clear limitations, it is not a bad place to start. We have only to recognize that the discoveries made here at this level may represent, borrowing from the cookery metaphor that runs through Tolkien's studies of OE verse-making, less the essential 'recipe' and more the light 'seasonings'.

The quest motif that Tolkien found so valuable may be one thing, but we should not forget the return journey. When Tolkien wryly quipped in 1961 of *The Lord of the Rings*' Swedish translator's ignorance of Beorhtnoth and the poem he had written about him – 'coming home dead without a head (as Beorhtnoth did) is not very delightful' – he could look back on more than a few awkward homecomings in his tales. 'But lock nor bar may hinder the homecoming spoken of old', declares Thorin (prematurely) to the men of Lake-town in *The Hobbit*. While the old prophecies, as Bilbo later notes, do come true after a fashion, Thorin is not around to enjoy them. Bilbo himself gets off fairly easy; unlike Beorhtnoth, Mr. Baggins is only 'Presumed Dead', returning in time to recover his house and most of his possessions from auction, though we are told that the 'legal bother ... lasted for years'. Frodo's return to the Shire in *The Lord of the Rings* is somewhat grimmer. On the heels of the miraculous completion of his quest at Mount Doom, he defines the ruffian-occupied Shire with tragic succinctness: 'Yes, this is Mordor'. And although the companions succeed in setting things right, Frodo soon 'dropped quietly out of all the doings of the Shire, and Sam was pained to notice how little honour he had in his own country'. Túrin, the tragic hero of *The Children of Húrin*, may fare worst of all. Returning to his mother's home in Dor-lómin, with his (and Morgoth's) work still unfinished, 'he came at last to the house that he sought. It stood empty and dark, and no living thing dwelt near it'. The mother and sister he sought there were long gone.

This may be mere 'seasoning', of course. If what we want is the recipe – to discover whether there is some core connection between these works, we can look to the questions posed by *The Homecoming*. Is war romantic or merely waste? How can war and sport be fused or confused? What makes a hero? What motivates him? Of what use is the Northern heroic spirit? Such questions are explored throughout Tolkien's legendarium.

The verse drama takes a hard look at them from the start. Whatever stirring action and brave deeds may have occurred, they are done. We find ourselves like Totta: alone with the dead in the dark. That eerie scene, the spent battlefield, is moving and disturbing in Tolkien's hands, and at times his attention seems to linger there longer and more vividly than it does on the great battles themselves. The last stand before the Black Gate fades from view almost before it begins, with Pippin crushed under the weight of a troll; but Gimli afterwards describes the search for his friend – 'the look of a hobbit's foot, though it be all that can be seen under a heap of bodies' – and effort of heaving 'that great carcase off' of him. We get no proper account of the Battle of Dagorlad – but we know the Dead Marshes, oh yes.

We see over and over the uneasy connection between war and sport: from the origins of the game of golf in *The Hobbit*, to the friendly orc-slaying wager between Gimli and Legolas at Helm's Deep. When Frodo draws first blood with Sting in Moria, Aragorn shouts encouragement – 'One for the Shire!' – as if tallying up the scoreboard. Like Beorhtnoth's sporting decision, both the allure and the peril of confusing the two are frequently on display. Faramir goes so far as to describe Gondor's decline in such terms: its people, he laments to Frodo and Sam, 'now love war and valour as things good in themselves, both a sport and an end'. We sense that such a decline has been long in the making, encouraged by those who might be expected to offer a better example. We learn in the Appendices of the brief reign of Eärnur, the last king of Gondor, nearly 1,000 years prior to Aragorn and the return of the king.

> He was a man of strong body and hot mood; but he would take no wife, for his only pleasure was in fighting, or in the exercise of arms. His prowess was such that none in Gondor could stand against him in those weapon-sports in which he delighted, seeming rather a champion than a captain or king.

Unwilling to abide the taunts of the Witch-king, he rides off with a 'small escort' to meet his foe in an ill-advised duel before Minas Morgul and is 'never heard of again', needlessly ushering in the era of the Stewards.

In his discourse with Frodo on the great tales and the boundless web of story by the Stairs of Cirith Ungol, Sam too notes such a confusion on the nature of adventure tales: 'I used to think that they were things the wonderful folk of the stories went out and looked for, because they wanted them, because they were exciting and life was a bit dull, a kind of a sport'. His realization points to the gulf between the actors in a drama and its audience, and the moral questions it poses. From the audience's perspective: the more dire the straits, the better the story. As Sam puts it, setting aside his distaste, 'even Gollum might be good in a tale'.

The critique of Beorhtnoth's conduct in 'Ofermod' turned the conversation on *The Battle of Maldon* away from the established notion of the poem's purely heroic quality and its celebration of the bonds of what the Roman historian Tacitus terms the *comitatus*: the band of retainers loyal to a lord unto death in battle. Yet in spite of his condemnation of Beorhtnoth's conduct, Tolkien is unequivocal in his admiration for the 'superb' heroism of those who chose to lay down their lives in love and loyalty. Just as Tída and Totta sing the praises of brave men like Ælfwine and Offa in 991, the *comitatus* motive is movingly expressed in the accounts of war in the legendarium. When Théoden falls from Snowmane on the Pelennor Fields and the Lord of the Nazgûl comes to gloat over his prey, the king is not 'utterly forsaken' though the 'knights of his house lay slain about him'. Éowyn still stands between them, undaunted, and it is she who fells the Nazgûl's monstrous winged steed. Merry, too, remembers his vows – 'King's man!' – though paralyzed by fear, his 'will made no answer' until he sees Éowyn's example, and his 'slow-kindled courage' rises, and together, against all odds, their loyalty to

Théoden (and their blades) make certain that the Lord of the Nazgûl is 'never heard again in that age of this world'.

The *comitatus* bond often overlaps with family ties as in the case of Éowyn and Théoden. The relationship between uncle and nephew – sister's son – Tolkien notes, is of particular historical and legendary importance. We recall that Thorin Oakenshield is not the only dwarf to fall in the Battle of the Five Armies, the young Fili and Kili join him: they 'had fallen defending him with shield and body, for he was their mother's elder brother'.

Such conduct would appear deeply ingrained in the cultures of Middle-earth. This is apparent in the iconic scene in which Gandalf holds the bridge of Khazad-dûm against the Balrog, commanding the rest of the fellowship to flee. The scene's likenesses to *The Battle of Maldon* have been discussed by scholars; Alexander M. Bruce has called it a kind of correction of Beorhtnoth at the causeway. Here Aragorn and Boromir are so reluctant to leave their leader's side with battle at hand as to be disobedient: they 'did not heed the command, but still held their ground'. Battle-cries raised, they rush to the wizard's aid, and it is only after his command is repeated – 'Fly, you fools!' – and he is gone into the abyss that they grudgingly obey, Aragorn leading the company now on the desperate escape from Moria.

On some level, these two may have preferred to tangle with the Balrog, and even fall with Gandalf – to express that Northern heroic spirit, the doctrine of doomed resistance summed up in *The Battle of Maldon* by the old member of the *comitatus*, Beorhtwold. From their first exchange at the Council of Elrond, almost an episode of flyting, Aragorn's grim assurance that both his sword and his sinews will be put 'to the test one day' echoes, as Tom Shippey notes, the stirring speech of Ælfwine in *Maldon*: 'Now may it be put to the test who is bold'.

Whether tied to bonds of loyalty, or duty to a mission, or that alloyed desire to make at least a good song, this desperate creed finds expression throughout *The Lord of the Rings*. During his turn as Ringbearer, Sam in fact is described in terms that quite plainly echo Beorhtwold's famous expression: when Frodo, presumed dead, is carried away by the orcs, Sam's 'weariness was growing but his will hardened all the more'. And in the final stages of the push toward Mount Doom, he finds himself transformed:

> But even as hope died in Sam, or seemed to die, it was turned to a new strength. Sam's plain hobbit-face grew stern, almost grim, as the will hardened in him, and he felt through all his limbs a thrill, as if he was turning into some creature of stone and steel that neither despair nor weariness nor endless barren miles could subdue.

Such shared ingredients are by no means confined only to *The Hobbit* and *The Lord of the Rings*. *Maldon* peeps through in the tradition of Isildur's death, told in the late narrative 'The Disaster of the Gladden Fields'. The king meets his end in the fatal waters of the river Anduin. As for the knights in Isildur's 'picked bodyguard', even their great shield-wall cannot long withstand the greater force of the orcs, and 'ere long they all lay dead, save one'. It is probably in the saga of Túrin Turambar that they are most prominent, as Richard C. West has suggested in his study of the theme of *ofermod* in that tale's long development. Túrin was reared on the aristocratic traditions much like Beorhtnoth and Torhthelm; his personal canon would include, among other legends, those recent tales of doomed resistance against Morgoth like Fingolfin's duel or his own father's last stand in the Battle of Unnumbered Tears. Túrin devotes his short unhappy life to redressing the wrongs done to his family by Morgoth. As hope – for peace, family, or victory – fades, his pride does not. And this pride, coupled with Morgoth's curse, will lead him from one disaster to the next. So he devotes himself wholly to the game of war, which he plays quite well – his prowess with sword and shield nearly unmatched. In Nargothrond he scorns even the Valar, and Beorhtwold's code of doomed resistance – where defeat, though inevitable, is no refutation – becomes for Túrin almost a religion. He looks to emulate his father, who, in his defiance of Morgoth has wrought a 'great deed' that death cannot undo, for it is 'written into the history of Arda'. In this high spirit, he manages to one-up even Beorhtnoth: *building* the bridge – and later refusing to cast it down – that soon enough speeds his enemies to the sack and ruin of Nargothrond.

Túrin does in fact go on to author one of the most audacious deeds of any Age; he will be remembered (vaguely) even late in the Third Age for his slaying of Glaurung: the prototypical hero, the first dragonslayer. Does he learn his lesson in the final confrontation with Glaurung, bringing willing companions (though they fail or fall in the end), opting for a tactically cunning approach instead of a sporting frontal assault? Are his misdeeds redeemed in this feat? Does Tolkien seek to reward his resistance via the strange prophecy of Mandos and a role to play in the Dagor Dagorath at the world's end? His legacy, like Beorhtnoth's, is open to interpretation. And while Tolkien wrote and rewrote Túrin's story at length and in brief, in verse and in prose, it is important to remember that the source material for this tale was intentionally withheld, as if lost to time. A legendary ur-text, The *Narn i Chîn Húrin*, is not, like *Maldon*, the extant fragment from a lost poet, but the lost poem from a named poet, Dírhavel. The verse form of this lost tale was said at least to resemble in some ways the old English alliterative metre, in which *Maldon* is written and in which Tolkien once experimented with Túrin's story, a project abandoned in the 1920s, though it gave rise also to what has been called 'the earliest *Silmarillion*'.

That *The Homecoming* and the legendarium share an essential ingredient in the concern with the wages of war and the ethics of combat will come as little surprise, but if it is indeed the recipe that we want, we must also consider how such ingredients are incorporated into the recipe's procedure. Here we find a connection that has received less attention: a large portion of *The Lord of the Rings* may be said to follow the same dialogic scheme of *The Homecoming*.

The debate of Tída and Totta ultimately transcends Beorhtnoth and the causeway, their perspectives come to represent a Quixotic contrast between fantasy and reality, romance and realism. Such perspectives are frequently contrasted in Tolkien's stories; it is hard not to think of *Maldon*, in fact, when Bilbo claims in *The Hobbit* that having 'heard songs of many battles' he has 'always understood that defeat may be glorious'. Bilbo struggles to square this view with his own experience having landed in such a battle – 'It seems very uncomfortable, not to say distressing'. Yet even the earthbound hobbit must admit to feeling 'splendid' about wearing a blade out of legend from Gondolin; and while that battle was 'the most dreadful of all Bilbo's experiences, and the one which at the time he hated most' it is, also, paradoxically 'the one he was most proud of, and most fond of recalling long afterwards'.

But in *The Lord of the Rings* these perspectives are baked into the essential structure of the story: like the voices of Tída and Totta, they alternate in tension from Book III to Book VI. With the departure of Boromir (another figure who has drawn comparison to Beorhtnoth) at the outset of *The Two Towers*, the fellowship is scattered, and the tale's simple quest narrative is rent apart, allowing Tolkien to show off his considerable aptitude for the medieval romance technique of interlacement. The many plot threads converging and diverging can be dizzying at times, but Tolkien boiled down the 'two main branches' thus: '1. Prime Action, the Ringbearers. 2. Subsidiary Action, the rest of the Company leading to the "heroic" matter'. In the latter branch, extending through Book III and Book V, we see Gandalf's miraculous return as the White Rider, the old magic of Fangorn Forest and the overthrow of the wizard Saruman and his Uruk-hai, our heroes tread the Paths of the Dead and ride to break the siege of Gondor. If the narrative remains hobbit-centric, if Merry and Pippin are our chief focal points, still we have an adventure that borders on sport: they pledge their swords as knights to kings and great lords, enjoy the spoils of war amidst the wreckage of Isengard, or ride like the wind atop Shadowfax with Gandalf at the reins.

In contrast, the journey of the Ringbearers recounted in Book IV and the early chapters of Book VI is of a different kind. As Frodo and Sam plod along (vaguely) toward a destination they can hardly fathom, they are led not by the Wise or the returning King but the wretched Gollum. They dress in Orc rags to escape detection; the battle-fields they traverse were fought upon thousands of years ago (though the muddy pools seem no less treacherous) and food, clean water, or an hour's rest all come to be like the rarest of luxuries. The contrast between the hobbits' experiences, if it were not already apparent, is hammered home upon reflection. Finding themselves back at long last on the borders of the Shire, Merry likens his adventure to a 'dream that has slowly faded'. But to Frodo, the return is 'more like falling asleep again'.

Thus when Tolkien wrote of *The Homecoming* reflecting the 'division of sympathy exhibited in *The Lord of the Rings*', he meant it. The keyword is 'division', for it captures both the essential structure of the narrative and the tensions between the two branches. C.S. Lewis's early reviews of his friend's great work praised this 'structural invention of the highest order', revelling in Tolkien's ability to locate a 'cool middle point between illusion and disillusionment'. While we might say that Tolkien seems to occupy the edges more than that cool centre between them, both of these texts do present a kind of synthesis in resolution. The heroic matter of the Captains of the West and their last stand before the Black Gate is of course subsidiary, no matter how many heroes they boast in their ranks. Yet that desperate – if not utterly hopeless – display of doomed resistance has still a part to play in bringing the quest to fruition. For Sauron is distracted, he does not register two hobbits and their tricksy guide creeping toward the Cracks of Doom until it is too late. Perhaps his head too is full of old lays concerning bright swords and kingly faces. Likewise, the recovery of Beorhtnoth's body requires the cooperation of both Tída and Totta. Without Tída, we might still find Totta with his teeth chattering among the dead. But on the other hand, without Totta's vim and sharp eyes, Tída surely would have blundered over the brink of the Blackwater.

I have said a word now on ingredients and procedure, but as Tolkien reminds us in his other great cookery metaphor from 'On Fairy-stories', we 'must not wholly forget the cooks'. Behind *The Homecoming*'s dramatic dialogue is Tolkien's search for the lost *Maldon* poet: Totta's terrifying journey through the battlefield, his long debate with Tída, and his mysterious dream serve up an imaginative genesis for the older poem, the last surviving fragment of Old English minstrelsy. Totta thus joins figures like Dírhavel, and Bilbo and Frodo – the long line of storytellers that both peoples and (we are told) produces Tolkien's tales. The runic scripts adorning the dust-jackets of *The Hobbit* and *The Lord of the Rings* identify Tolkien only as a compiler or translator of these ancient works, the last link in the kind of long chains of transmission he explores in 'The Tradition of Versification in Old English'. *The Homecoming* and *The Lord of the Rings* are both ultimately stories about stories. It is the poets – the cooks – who bear the heavy burden of preserving fact and fiction, history and legend. Our later understanding of these is heavily influenced by the shape they give their poems and stories.

And finally it is in the hands of the reader, whose freedom Tolkien was at pains to defend. Can we hear the tears through the harp's twanging? Do we take up the voice in the dark's appeal to listen for a while? The proof of the pudding, we might say, is in the reading.

When Totta laments that 'the songs wither, and the world worsens', he recalls in a way Treebeard's lesson, after telling Merry and Pippin the sad story of the Entwives: 'songs like trees bear fruit only in their own time and their own way: and sometimes they are withered untimely'. We may be grateful for poets like Totta, and for the unlikely chance survival of their words, conspiring to give us the *Maldon* fragment, and Beorhtwold's unforgettable code, and finally helping to produce *The Homecoming of Beorhtnoth* and *The Lord of the Rings*, too.

BIBLIOGRAPHY

Atherton, Mark. *There and Back Again: J.R.R. Tolkien and the Origins of* The Hobbit. London: I.B. Tauris. 2012.

———. *The Battle of Maldon: War and Peace in Tenth-Century England.* London: Bloomsbury. 2021.

Bruce, Alexander M. 'Maldon and Moria: On Byrhtnoth, Gandalf, and Heroism in *The Lord of the Rings*'. *Mythlore* 26, no. 1, art. 11. 2007.

Bowman, Mary R. 'Refining the Gold: Tolkien, The Battle of Maldon, and the Northern Theory of Courage'. *Tolkien Studies* 7. 2010. 91–115.

Carpenter, Humphrey. *J.R.R. Tolkien: A Biography.* London: HarperCollins. 1977.

Deegan, Marilyn and Stanley Rubin. 'Byrhtnoth's Remains: A Reassessment of his Stature' in *The Battle of Maldon AD 991.* D.G. Scragg. Oxford: Blackwell. 1991.

Drout, Michael D.C. 'J.R.R. Tolkien's Medieval Scholarship and its Significance'. *Tolkien Studies*, vol. 4. 2007. 113–76.

Eddison, E.R. (Trans.). *Egil's Saga.* London: HarperCollins. 2014.

Fisher, Jason. 'J.R.R. Tolkien: The Foolhardy Philologist'. *A Wilderness of Dragons: Essays in Honor of Verlyn Flieger.* John D. Rateliff, ed. Wayzata: Gabbro Head. 2018.

Gordon, E.V., ed. *The Battle of Maldon.* London: Methuen. 1937.

Grybauskas, Peter. 'Dialogic War: From the Battle of Maldon to the War of the Ring'. *Mythlore* 29, no. 3. 2011. 37–56.

———. 'A Portrait of the Poet as a Young Man: Omission in

The Homecoming of Beorhtnoth' in *A Sense of Tales Untold: Exploring the Edges of Tolkien's Literary Canvas*. Kent: Kent State University Press. 2021.

Hammond, Wayne G., and Christina Scull. *Chronology. The J. R. R. Tolkien Companion and Guide*. London: Harper-Collins. 2017.

Holmes, John R. 'The Battle of Maldon' in *J. R. R. Tolkien Encyclopedia: Scholarship and Critical Assessment*. Michael D. C. Drout, ed. New York: Routledge. 2007. 52–4.

Honegger, Thomas. 2007. *'The Homecoming of Beorhtnoth*: Philology and the Literary Muse'. *Tolkien Studies* 4: 189–99.

Lee, Stuart. 'Lagustreamas: The Changing Waters Surrounding J. R. R. Tolkien and *The Battle of Maldon*' in *The Wisdom of Exeter: Anglo-Saxon Studies in Honor of Patrick W. Conner*. E. J. Christie, ed. Kalamazoo: Medieval Institute Publications. 2020. 157–75.

Lewis, C.S. 'Tolkien's The Lord of the Rings' in *On Stories and Other Essays on Literature*. San Francisco: Harcourt. 1982. 83–90.

Mills, A.D. *A Dictionary of British Place-Names*. Oxford: Oxford University Press. 2003.

Parker, Eleanor. 2018. '"Merry sang the monks": Cnut's Poetry and the *Liber Eliensis*'. *Scandinavica*, vol. 57, no. 1. 2018.

Shippey, Tom. *The Road to Middle-earth*. London: Harper-Collins. 2005.

——. 'Tolkien and the Homecoming of Beorhtnoth' in *Roots and Branches: Selected Papers on Tolkien*. Zollikofen: Walking Tree, 2007. 323–39.

Smol, Anna. 'Bodies in War: Medieval and Modern Tensions in "The Homecoming"' in *'Something Has Gone Crack': New Perspectives on J.R.R. Tolkien in the Great War*. Janet Brennan Croft and Annika Röttinger, eds. Zollikofen: Walking Tree. 2019.

Stenton, Frank. *Anglo-Saxon England*. Third Edition. Oxford: Clarendon Press. 1971.

Tolkien, Christopher. 'Note on the Text' in *The Lay of Aotrou and Itroun*. J.R.R. Tolkien. Verlyn Flieger, ed. London: HarperCollins. 2016.

Tolkien, J.R.R. *The Letters of J. R. R. Tolkien*. Humphrey Carpenter, ed., with Christopher Tolkien. London: Harper-Collins. 1981.

——. *Finn and Hengest*. Alan Bliss, ed. London: HarperCollins. 1982.

——. 'Beowulf: The Monsters and the Critics' in *The Monsters and the Critics and Other Essays*. Christopher Tolkien, ed. London: HarperCollins. 1983. 5–48.

——. 'On Fairy-stories' in *The Monsters and the Critics and Other Essays, edited by Christopher Tolkien*. London: HarperCollins. 1983, 109–61.

——. *The Hobbit*. Boston: Houghton Mifflin. 1994.

——. *The Lays of Beleriand. The History of Middle-earth I*. Christopher Tolkien, ed. London: HarperCollins. 2002.

——. *The Treason of Isengard. The History of Middle-earth II*. Christopher Tolkien, ed. London: HarperCollins. 2002.

——. *The Peoples of Middle-earth. The History of Middle-earth III*. Christopher Tolkien, ed. London: HarperCollins. 2002.

——. *The Fellowship of the Ring. The Lord of the Rings*. London: HarperCollins. 2005.

——. *The Return of the King. The Lord of the Rings*. London: HarperCollins. 2005.

——. *The Two Towers. The Lord of the Rings*. London: Harper-Collins. 2005.

——. *Unfinished Tales of Númenor and Middle-earth*. Christopher Tolkien, ed. London: HarperCollins. 2006.

——. *The Children of Húrin*. Christopher Tolkien, ed. London: HarperCollins. 2007.

—. *The Fall of Arthur*. Christopher Tolkien, ed. London: Harper-Collins. 2013.

——. *Beowulf: A Translation and Commentary*. Christopher Tolkien, ed. London: HarperCollins. 2014.

——. 'Dragons'. *The Hobbit*. Deluxe Edition. Commemorative Booklet. London: HarperCollins. 2018.

——. *The Nature of Middle-earth*. Carl F. Hostetter, ed. London: HarperCollins. 2021.

——. *MS. Tolkien 5*. Tolkien Papers. Bodleian Library, Univ. of Oxford. N.d.

——. *MS. Tolkien A 30/2*. Tolkien Papers, Bodleian Library, Univ. of Oxford. N.d.

——. *MS. Tolkien A 38/1*. Tolkien Papers, Bodleian Library, Univ. of Oxford. N.d.

——. *MS. Tolkien Drawings 88*. Tolkien Papers, Bodleian Library, Univ. of Oxford. N.d.

——. *MS. 1952/2/1 'The Home-coming of Beorhtnoth Beorhthelm's Son'*. Tolkien-Gordon Archive. Special Collections, University of Leeds. N.d.

West, Richard C. 'Canute and Beorhtnoth' in *A Wilderness of Dragons: Essays in Honor of Verlyn Flieger*. John D. Rateliff, ed. Wayzata: Gabbro Head, 2018. 335–58.

——. 'Túrin's Ofermod: An Old English Theme in the Development of the Story of Túrin' in *Tolkien's Legendarium*. Verlyn Flieger and Carl F. Hostetter, eds. 2000.

Yates, Jessica. 'The Influence of William Morris on J.R.R. Tolkien'. Tolkien 2005: The Ring Goes Ever On. Conference Paper. 2005.